Some Economic Aspects of India-
Forestry and Industr

Some Economic Aspects of India—Agriculture, Forestry and Industry

DR. B.T. RAMAPPA

HEAD, DEPT. OF ECONOMICS
TUNGA MAHAVIDYALAYA
THIRTHAHALLI-577432
KUVEMPU UNIVERSITY
KARNATAKA

SERIALS PUBLICATIONS
NEW DELHI (INDIA)

First Published – 2011

ISBN: 978-81-8387-446-5

Published by

SERIALS PUBLICATIONS
4830/24, 1st Floor, Ansari Road
Darya Ganj, New Delhi-110002 (India)
Phone : 23245225. Fax : 91-11-23272135
E-mail : serials@sify.com
serialspublications.india@gmail.com
Website : www.serialspublications.com

Preface

Even since the inception of planning, Agriculture plays a pivotal role in the economic development of the Indian Economy. It is an accelerating force in the Economic take-off. The progress and problems of the sector are presented in the paper and possible solutions have been pointed out in the people. Forestry has been treated as a part of Agriculture. Industry great emphasis has been laid on the development of the Small Scale Industrial Sector (SSIs). Infact, the SSI sector has been expected to play a crucial role in the industrial development of the country. Indeed, the growth of the industries in this sector has been a dominant feature of our economic development since independence. It is estimated that this sector accounts for about 40 percent of the total industrial output and contributes about 35 percent of the total direct exports. As far as employment is concerned, it comes next only to agriculture.

The Government(Central and States) have taken a number of measures to solve the age-old problems of these industries, such as lack of credit facilities, outmoulded methods and techniques absence of organized marketing, unsatisfactory arrangements for the supply of raw materials and competition from large –scale units. Apart from these, credit facilities are made available to these industries through a number of institutions. Industrial estates and rural industrial projects have been set up, and industries co-operatives have been organized.

After implementation of liberalization policy, the SSI sector is facing critical problems for the sustainable development. It is the right time to discuss the different outcome of this policy. On "status of SSI during the period of post Liberalization." Therefore, national level seminar had been organized for the discussion about the above theme. The present publication is to focus the present status, problems of the SSIs under the globalize condition and to suggest the suitable policy implications for the development of SSIs (SMEs) in India.

I am immensely grateful to Dr. M.G. Basava Raja, Director and Professor of Economic, Sir M. Virvesvaraya, P.G. Centre, University of Mysore, Mandya. I am highly grateful to Dr. Mahendra Kumar, Reader, Deptt. of Economics and Cooperation. Manasagangotri, University of Mysore, Mysore. I am also grateful to Dr. H.R. Krishnaiah Gowda, Managing Director, District Cooperative Central Bank, Hassan, for their encouragement and support. The support of my wife Mrs. H.K.Suma and my children kumari B.R. Deepthi and B.R.Thrupthi helped me to complete this work. Finally, my sincere thanks to the Serial Publishers and Distributors, Delhi for their keen interest in publishing the book.

B.T. RAMAPPA

List of Abbreviations

KEB	Karnataka Electricity Board
KIADB	Karnataka Industrial Area Development Board
SEF	Small Enterprises Firms
SSIs	Small Scale Industries
KSSIDC	Karnataka State Small Industries Development Corporation
DIC	District Industries Centre
WTO	World Trade Organization
SIDO	Small Industry Development Organisation
EOUs	Export Oriented Units
SMEs	Small and Medium Enterprises
DFPAs	District Enterprise Promotion Agencies
NEP	New Economic Policy
LPG	Liberalization, Privatization, Globalization
KSSIIDC	Karnataka Small Industries Investment Development Corporation
KPTCL	Karnataka Power Transmission Company Ltd.
SSSEs	Small Scale Service Establishment
MNCs	Multinational Corporation
GATT	General Agreement Trade and Tariff
TRIPs	Trade related Intellectual property Rights
SEZs	Special Economic Zones
VITC	Visvesvaraya Industrial Trade Centre
SIDF	Small Industries Development Fund
NEF	National Equity Fund
SIDBI	Small Industries Development Bank of India
KSFC	Karnataka State Finance Corporation
CGFS	Credit Guarantee Fund Scheme

CLCSS	Credit Linked Capital Subsidy Scheme
IDBI	Industrial Development Bank of India
STPI	Software Technology Park of India
LDCs	Less Developed Countries
EDPs	Entrepreneurship Development Programme
SWA	Single Window Agency
CDA	Cluster Development Approach
BA	Boilers Act
BKP	Bio-technology Knowledge Park
GC	Growth Centres
AEP	Apparel Export Parks
PAS	Purchase Assistance Scheme
HPAS	Hire Purchase Assistance Scheme
SIEIA	Stick Industries Environment Impact Assessment
EMP	Environment Management Plans
UPTECH	Technology UP-gradation and Management
ICTI	Information and Communications Technology Infrastructure
KSSIMC	Karnataka State Small Industries Marketing Corporation
NCAER	National Council of Applied Economic Research
FNF	Friedrich Neumann Foundation
CII	Confederation of India Industry
HRD	Human Resource Development
EU	European Union
TRIPs	Intellectual Property Rights
TBT	Technical Barriers to Trade
TSIs	Thrust Sector Industries
EOUs	Export Oriented Units
CGS	Credit Guarantee Scheme
SIDF	Small Industry Development Fund
NEFS	National Equity Fund Scheme
SCA	Seed Capital Assistance

Contents

Preface	*v*
Abbreviation	*vii*
Articles	*Page No*
1. Impact of Liberalization and Globalization on Small Scale Industry in India	1-13
2. Impact of World Trade Organization and Its Rules and Regulations	14-29
3. Necessary Finance for Small Scale Industries in India	30-48
4. A Critical View of the Industrial Policy of Karnataka Since 1982-2011:(Particular Reference to Small Scale Industries)	49-62
5. Industrial Policy of Karnataka - 2006-11 —A Critical Review	63-73
6. Present Scenario of Small Scale Industries in Karnataka	74-90
7. Entrepreneurship in a Globalizing Economy	91-99
8. Imbalance in the Growth of SSIs in Mysore District —The Policy Needs	100-108
9. State Level Economic Reforms – with Special Reference to Infrastructure Sector of Karnataka	109-127
10. The Third Sector Participation in Social	

Forestry - A Felt Need in India 128-134

11. Social Forestry and Role in Rural Development 135-141

12. Agriculture Marketing in Karnataka: —An Analysis of Problems and Improvement Programmes 142-154

13. Natural Resource Management in Sustainable Agriculture 155-167

14. The Inter–Linking Rivers Project —A Useful Plan for Growth and Not a Mindless Dream 168-178

15. Agrarian Distress and Alleviatory measures: 179-190

16. Contract Farming in India 191-203

CHAPTER 1

Impact of Liberalisation and Globalisation on Small Scale Industry in India

Introduction

Economic Liberalization is considered as an important element in the reform package. The main aim of the new industrial policy of 1991 was to achieve sustained growth in productivity, self-reliance, gainful employment and growth with equity. The proponents of new economic policy of 1991 were of the conviction that Liberalisation, Privatization and Globalization (LPG) would usher in healthy competition, which in turn lead to productivity improvements and higher growth.

The strategy of economic development of any country that formulates programmes for removal poverty of the people by providing large scale employment, education and training, capital formation, effective mobilization of resources, balanced economic growth, expansion of trade, transport and equitable distribution of national income with effective involvement and participation of all its citizens in the accomplishment of the goal, cannot neglect Small Scale Industrial Sector (SSI).

It is an accepted truth that the comprehensive balanced growth mainly depends upon two major sectors, such as Agriculture and Industry. In the Industrial sector the SSI constitutes a very important segment. It is true with regard to Indian economy also. The Indian economy during Five Year (FY) 2005, the SSI sector is estimated to have recorded a growth of 13.5 percent in the output at current prices and 8.1 percent at constant prices as compared to 14.7 percent and 8.6 percent respectively in the previous year. As per the estimates, the production in the SSI sector, at current prices, is estimated to be at Rs 4,07,630 crore during the year 2004 – 05 from Rs. 3,57,733 crore in the previous year. The number of units in SSI sector is estimated to have increased to 118.59 Lakh units at the end of March 2005(FY, both

Registered &Non- Registered) as compared to 113.95 Lakh units at the end of March 2004(FY). Employment in the sector is anticipated at the level of 282 .91 Lakh at the end of March 2005 expanded during the year, with an addition of 11.44 Lakh persons, to the sector's aggregate employment of 271.47 Lakh at the end of March 2004. The exports from the SSI sector surged from $ US 14, 938 million during FY 2002, to $ US 17,773 million during FY 2003. This is very clear by the comments made in "Raising Finance for Small Enterprise Development" a publication of **UNIDO** (1997). It runs as that SSI, being labour – intensive, to provide employment and earning opportunities for unskilled workers. Research in six developing countries shows that, collectively small establishments account for most industrial employment, particularly in less developed countries (LDCs), much manufacturing employment is found in rural areas. At the early stages of development, Small Enterprises are predominately craft based are located mainly in rural areas to meet local demands. At later stages of development, grow into or replaced between modern small enterprises with a larger market potential and higher quality products and benefits of economies of scale.

Some light is thrown on the impact of these policies on SSIs by the remarks made by some authors. The present era is characterized by two policies- Liberalization and Globalization. Kumar and Philip (2005) in their study on "Intellectual Property Rights; Implications for the Small scale Industry in India" observed, New Economic Policy coupled with the New International Trade Regime characterized by the WTO, ushered in an era of Liberalization and Globalization. In its wake, SSIs lost the shield of protective policies and have been exposed to the onslaught of large organizations and International competition. Murthy's (2004) study on "Small Scale Industries and Entrepreneurial Development" says that SSI sector plays a pivotal role in the Indian economy in terms of employment after independence inspite of stiff competition failed by them with large sectors. But, according to Murthy, it has not received enough encouraging support form the government. However; these remarks do not give us a comprehensive picture on the impact of Liberalization and Globalization on SSI in India. The insufficiency on the study of SSIs after the policy of Liberalization and Globalization put to operation in the country is an utmost importance. With this it is possible to understand the present status of SSI sector, on the basis of which it becomes easier to evolve suitable policy measures to augment the accelerated growth of the sector.

This study is mainly related to Modern Small Scale Industries in India, based on Secondary data. Modern Small Scale Industries are based on intermediate technology, both labour intensive and as well as capital intensive. These industries are classified on the basis of their investment limit – Small-scale Industries and Ancillary industries (Maximum Limit-Rs 1crore) and Tiny sector units (Maximum Limit Rs 25 Lakhs).This study requires a penetration in to different aspects of the policy matters such as the contents of W.T.O. agreement. Industrial policy adopted after the WTO agreement. Ultimately their impact on the SSI sector. This necessitates the study of different faces of SSIs in the country.

WTO Agreement

The WTO, established in January 1995, is one of the Key outcomes of the 1986- 94. Uruguay Round of multilateral trade negotiations. In particular Uruguay Round gave rise to two new multilateral agreements. The general agreement on trade in services (GATS) and the agreement on Trade related aspects of Intellectual Property Right (TRIPRs) agreement cover forms a trade and also issues previously outside the scope of the GATT. A Multilateral agreement is binding only on countries that sign the agreement.

In 1947 October a formal body GATT was initiated. When GATT Members did not ratify ITO. Later it was institutionalized as WTO and the responsibility of monitoring the administrating was entrusted to a small secretarial established at Geneva. Initially GATT evolved two key principles-Article-1 (i.e. Non-discrimination), Artcle-2-(National Treatment). The purpose of ratification is to make the level of protection afforded by NTBs (National Trade Barriers) transparent, and also comparable to tariff rates, for the ultimate purpose of negotiating their reduction. Between 1947-62 several rounds of tariff negotiations took place. In the sixth round known as Kennedy round arrived at a common policy in reducing tariff.

Later Uruguay round launched in 1986 and concluded on 15th April 1994. Further elaborated the agreement including even agricultural production, textiles, Trade services, investment, intellectual property rights etc.

Industrial Policies Adopted after the WTO

To say the policy of Liberalization and Globalization was accepted even though, GATT/WTO member countries are not used the particular words. As a result of this in India also policy changes took place. With regarded to the SSI sector also it is true.

New Industrial Policy, 1991

SSIs under a liberalized regime constrained by a number of factors, among which the more important are as follows:

1. Change in consumer preference.
2. Out moulded technology
3. Uneconomic scales of operation
4. Lack of organization
5. Total disregard of environment standards, and
6. High incidence of sickness. In a partial response to this situation, the government announced on August 6, 1991, a joint package of policy measure, for small, tiny, handloom, handicraft and village industries. It has proposed clear guidelines to deal with the three major areas of concern for the sector.
   1. Finance 2. Marketing 3. Technology

The Industrial policy of 1991 was accompanied by a special policy statement for SSIs whose main features were,

1. To impart greater vitality and growth to the sector, it would be deregulates and debureaucratised.
2. Modification in all statements, regulations and procedures to ensure, they do not go against the interest of small and village enterprises.
3. Separate package for promoting tiny units and recognition of all industry related service and business enterprises at SSI.
4. To shift emphasis from subsidized / cheap credit except for specified target groups to ensure adequate flow of credit on normative basis.

5. To provide access to capital market by allowing 24percent equity participation by other industrial undertakings.
6. Legislation to ensure prompt payment of bills and legislation for Limited Partnership Act.
7. Introduction of a new scheme of Integrated Infrastructure Development to promote industrialization in rural and backward areas.
8. Stress technology up gradation by setting up a Technology Development Cell and strengthening the facilities available with SIDO (Small Industries Development Organization), and enforcement of quality control.
9. Promotion of marketing of SSI products through institutions, other agencies and consortia approach and ancillarisation.
10. Promotion of exports by setting up export development centre.
11. Change in definition of women's enterprises and support to women entrepreneurs.
12. Significant expansion in programmes for entrepreneurship.

New Industrial Policy, 1998

On June 25, 1998 the Government announcement a package of policy initiatives to extent much demanded succor by the SSI sector. It includes as follows:

1. Frequency of checks reduced from weekly to monthly.
2. Periodicity of audit limited to once in two years as against discretionary
3. No coercive action to realize excise dues pending court order.
4. Excise refund claims to be disposed off within three months" reasonability to be fixed.
5. Units clearing goods up to Rs. 40 Lakh exempted form filing mandatory declaration of goods produced.

August 2000 Package

This based on the recommendations of S.P. Gupta committee and other inputs from various sources a package of measures were announced with a view to preparing the SSI sector to meet global competition.

1. 15 items short – listed for degeneration.
2. Hike in investment limit to Rs. Five crore for 41 items, as compared to Rs. One crore for the rest of the SSI sector.

The gradual liberalization on this front is based on the Chinese model producing huge volume at highly competitive prices.

In new measures were announced on August 30, 2000

1. Excise exemption limit rose to Rs. One crore
2. 12 percent capital subsidy for investment in technology in selected sector;
3. Credit Guarantee Scheme with Rs. 125 crore corpus;
4. Composite loan limit rose to Rs. 25 lakh.
5. Rs 441 crore scheme for khadi and village industries.

Some of the important policy initiatives taken during 2004–05 for SSI sector include the following

1. Eighty-five items reserved for exclusive manufacture in the small scale sector were dereserved in October 2004. Further, 108 items were dereserved in March 2005. With these dereservations, the number of items reserved for exclusive manufacture in the SSI sector stand at 506. (presently-326)
2. To facilitate technology upgradation and enhancing competitiveness, the investment limit in plant and machinery in respect of Seven items of sport goods was raised from Rs. One crore to Rs. Five crore in October 2004.
3. Composite loan limit for SSI sector was increased from Rs. 50 lakh to Rs. One crore by the RBI.
4. The National Commission on Enterprises in the unorganized/informal sector was set up in september 2004. The commission will, Inter – Asia, recommend measures considered necessary for improvement in the productivity of these enterprises, generation of large scale employment opportunities on a sustainable basis, linkage of the sector to institutional.

5. Industrial policy would promote projects, which are organized in close co-operation on the basis of joint ownership. Growers will be encouraged to set up processing units within the framework of Cooperative Societies. This will also ensure the transmission of better technology for enhanced agricultural production.
6. Agro processing industries would receive high priority in credit allocation from the financial institutions.

Impact on the Small Scale Industrial Sector

Table 1: Growth pattern of Small Scale Industrial Sector. (Before Liberalization 1980-81 to 1990-91)

Year	*No. of Units (Lakhs Nos)*	*Production (Rs. Crores)*	*Employment (Lakh Nos)*	*Export (Rs. Crores)*
1980-81	8.74	28060	71.00	1643
1981-82	9.62	32600	75.00	2071
1982-83	10.59	35000	79.00	2045
1983-94	11.55	41620	84.15	2164
1984-85	12.40	50520	90.00	2541
1985-86	13.53	61228	96.00	2769
1986-87	14.62	72250	101.40	3643
1987-88	15.83	87300	107.00	4372
1988-89	17.12	106400	113.00	5489
1989-90	18.23	132320	119.60	7625
1990-91	19.48	155340	125.30	9664
AM	13.79	75967.09	96.5	4002.36
CGR	8.33	19.22	5.97	18.64

Source: DC, SSIs(2000), SSI in India. The growth sector for the millennium, New delhi: SIDO Ministry of SSIs. Annual Reports of SIDO for 1992-93 to 2003-04, Government of India, New Delhi. SIDBI (2004-05), Annual Report Small Industries Development Bank of India.

The above table shows that the numerical figures shown in the Table No 1 is made more illustrious and easy understandable by the graph given. Hence it requires number verbal explanation.

Graph 1: Growth, No of units and Employment (values in lakhs)

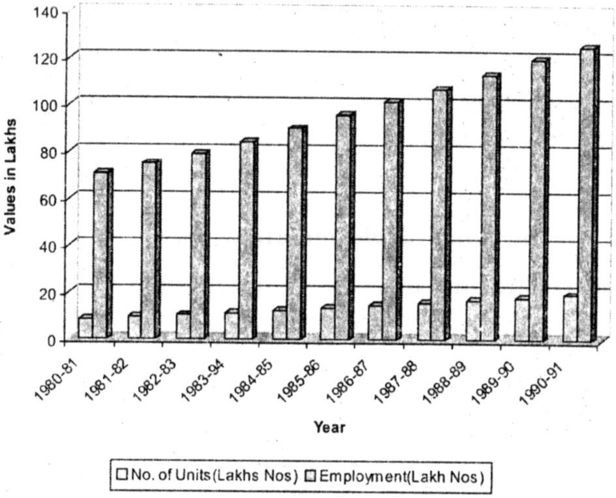

Table 2: Impact of Liberalization on Small Scale Industrial Sector. (1991-92 to 2002-03)

Year	*No. Of Units (Lakhs Nos)*	*Production (Rs. Crores)*	*Employment (Lakh Nos)*	*Export (Rs. Crores)*
1991-92	20.82	1,78,699	129.80	13,883
1992-93	22.86	2,09,300	134.06	17,785
1993-94	23.81	2,41,678	139.38	25,307
1994-95	25.71	2,93,990	146.56	29,068
1995-96	27.24	3,56,213	152.61	36,470
1996-97	28.57	4,12,636	160.00	39,249
1997-98	30.14	4,65,171	167.20	44,437
1998-99	31.21	5,27,515	171.58	49,481
1999-00	32.25	5,78,470	177.30	54,200
2000-01	33.7	6,39,024	185.64	69,797
2001-02	34.64	6,90,522	192.23	71,244
2002-03	35.1	8,24,363	200.79	86,103
AM	28.84	411881.75	163.1	44752
CGR	4.84	11.89	4.07	17

Source: DC, SSIs(2000), SSI in India. The growth sector for the millennium, New Delhi: SIDO Ministry of SSIs • Annual Reports of SIDO for 1992-93 to 2003-04, Government of India, New Delhi. • SIDBI (2004-05), Annual Report Small Industries Development Bank of India.

The above table shows that the changes took place from 1991-92 to 2002-03 in number of units, production, employment and exports, the variations appears to be positive. The rate of growth is not as required in certain aspects. This is made clearer by the graphical illustration given.

Graph 2: Growth - Production and Export

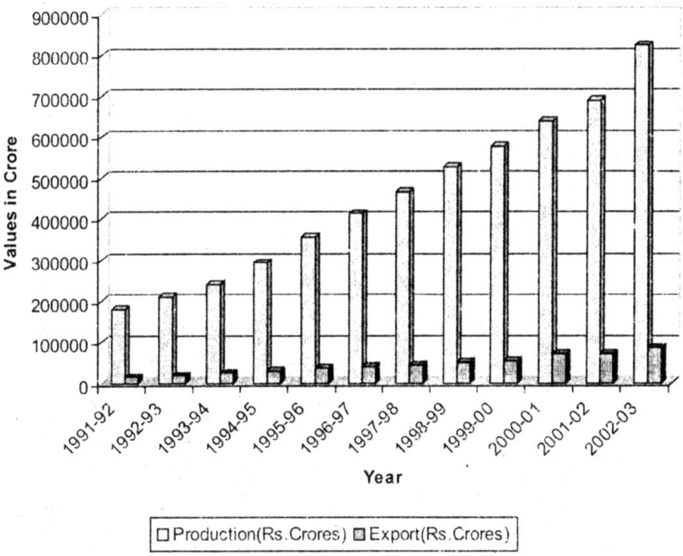

Table: I$2 Growth Pattern of SSIs (in lakh)

During the last ten years of Pre-EL (Economic Liberalization) period, the number of SSIs increased from 8.74 Lakhs (in 1980-81), to 19.48 Lakhs (in 1990-91) (VIDE TABLE 1&2). There was, thus 2.65 times increase in the number of SSI units in the country. The Compound Growth Rate (CGR) was 8.33 percent. During the Post-EL period (i.e., from 1991-92 to 2002-03), the number of SSIs increased from 20.82 Lakhs to 35.10 Lakh, there was thus, 1.84 times increase in the number of SSIs in the country. During these ten years, the CGR was 4.84 percent. It means Post EL period declined the CGR (units).

Table: I&2 Growth Pattern of Production in SSIs (Rs in Crores)

The production of SSIs in 1980-81 was Rs 28060 crores, which increased to Rs 155340 crores in 1990-91. During ten years of pre EL period, there was 9.48 times increased, and the CGR of production was 19.22 percent. During the Post EL period, production increased from Rs 178699 crores in 1991-92, to Rs 824363 in 2002-03. The CGR of production was 11.89 percent. After EL period declined the production of SSIs.

Table: I&2 Growth Patterns of Employment in SSIs (in Lakh).

During the ten years of Pre- EL period, the number of persons employed in SSIs increased from 71.00 Lakh in 1980-81 to 125.30 Lakhs in 1990-91, which represents 1.96 times increase in employment in SSIs. The CGR of employment was 5.97 percent.During the Post-EL period, the number of persons employed in SSIs increased from 129.80 Lakhs in 1991-92 to 200.79 Lakhs in 2002-03, which represents 1.61 times increase in employment in SSIs. The CGR of Employment was 4.07 percent. Post EL period substantial declined in Employment.

Table 3: Share of SSI in total export (% age share)

1971-72	9.6	1980-81	24.5	1990-91	29.7
72-73	15.5	81-82	26.5	91-92	31.5
73-74	15.6	82-83	23.0	92-93	33.3
74-75	16.2	83-84	21.9	93-94	36.4
75-76	13.2	84-85	22.1	94-95	35.2
76-77	14.9	85-86	25.4	95-96	34.3
77-78	15.4	86-87	29.0	96-97	33.4
78-79	18.7	87-88	27.8	97-98	35.2
79-80	19.0	88-89	27.0	98-99	34.6
		89-90	27.5	99-00	33.9

Source: • DC, SSIs(2000), SSI in India. The growth sector for the millennium, New delhi: SIDO Ministry of SSIs •Annual Reports of SIDO for 1992-93 to 2003-04, Government of India, New Delhi. •SIDBI (2004-05), Annual Report Small Industries Development Bank of India.

Table- I, 2&3 Growth Pattern of Exports in SSIs (Rs in crores)

Table-1, 2&3 the data on the exports of SSIs are available up to 2002-03.The values of exports of SSIs increased from Rs 1643 crores in 1980-81 to Rs 9664 crores in 1990-91. There was thus 1.82 times increase in the Exports. The CGR in this period was 18.64 percent.During the Post EL period, the value of exports increased from 1991-92, Rs 13,883 crores to Rs 86103 crores in 2002-03, which represents 6.91 percent increase in the value of Exports. The CGR in this period was 17 percent. In the Post – EL period marginal declined in the value of exports.

Table 4: Sickness in SSI sector

Year	*No. of Sick Units*	*Year*	*No. of Sick Units*
1981	25342	1991-92	245575
1982	58551	1992-93	238176
1983	78363	1993-94	256452
1984	91450	1994-95	268815
1985	117783	1995-96	262376
1986	145776	1996-97	235032
1987	204255	1997-98	221536
1988	240573	1998-99	306221
1989-90	218828	1999-00	304235
1990-91	271472	2000-01	249630
AM	145239.3	AM	258804.8
CGR	26.51	CGR	1.25

Source: • DC, SSIs(2000), SSI in India. The growth sector for the millennium, New delhi: SIDO Ministry of SSIs • Annual Reports of SIDO for 1992-93 to 2003-04, Government of India, New Delhi. •SIDBI (2004-05), Annual Report Small Industries Development Bank of India.

Graph: 3 Sick Units of SSIs

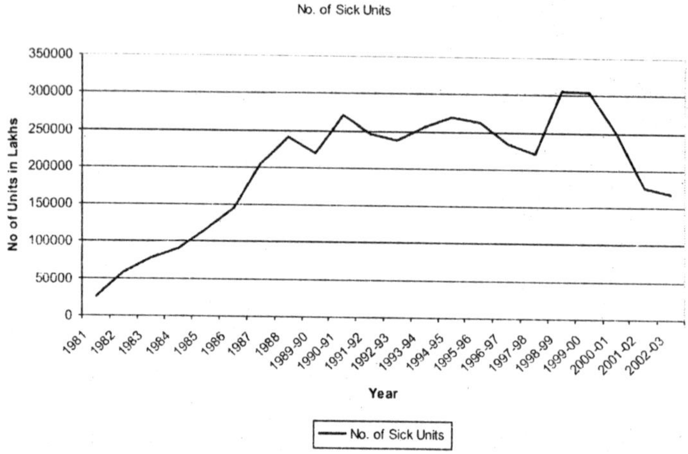

Growth of Sick SSIs During Pre-El and Post-El Periods

As shown in the table no 4 and Graph no 3 of sick units went on increasing formidable from 1981 to 1988 later the figure does not show a formidable variation till 1988-99. Afterwards the number of sick units has been showing a decreasing trend. But this cannot be taken as a positive growth in the sector. Because it might be the influence of several other factors. During ten years of Pre-EL period, the number of sick SSIs increased from 25,342 (in 1980-81) to 2, 71,472 Lakh (in 1990-91). There was thus, 10.56 times increase in the number of sick SSIs in the country. The CGR was 26.51 percent.

During EL period, the incidence of sickness (according to RBI figures) has decreased. As given in Table 1,2&4, the number of sick SSIs has decreased from 245575 in 1991-92 to 249630 in 2000-01 i.e., 0.68times decrease in the number of sick SSIs. The CGR of sick SSIs is also remarkable less 1.25 percent. The arithmetical illustrations given in Table 4 nullify the hue and cry about EL.

Conclusion

The comparative pictures of the above data as show that the industrial policies evolved by the Government of India put the whole SSI sector in to a hot water. This is purely because of the policy of the Liberalization and Globalization put to operation indiscrimately. In order to bring about even distribution of SSI's in different regions of the country, to encourage and help prospective persons to establish SSIs in the backward areas. The only way to liberate the SSI in the country is to evolve a policy of easy credit, marketing, Tax free period, Reservation of products for manufacturing, De-licensing, Lessening of bueracrating control, upgradition of technology etc

References

1. GATT (1991), "Trade Policy Review Mechanism, European Communities March, Geneva: GATT.
2. Soundarapandian.M and Rajkumar.C. (2003) "Impact of New Economic Policy on Small Scale Industries" *Dominant Publishers New Delhi. 86—92*
3. Reserve Bank of India (1997), "Report of the Expert Committee on Small Enterprises", *Supplement to RBI Bulletin, Bombay, Sept 48&49.*
4. Reddy T.S. and Reddy L.V. (1988), "Sickness in Small Industries" *Himalaya publishing House, Delhi".*
5. Hindley, B. (1994), "Safeguards, VERs and Antidumping Actions," *in OECD documents, The New World Trading System (Paris:OECD), 91- 103.*
6. Jackson. (1969), World Trade and the Law of the GATT *(Indianpolis: Bobbs MerrillRajender Kumar and Philip P.J(2005), "Intellectual Property Rights: Implications For The Small Scale Industries In India", Political Economy Journal of India, 14(121).*
7. Dr. Syed Vazith Hussain (2003), "Small Scale Industries in the New Millennium" Published by prabhat Kumar Sharma for Sarup and Sons, Delhi P No. – 29
8. Development Commissioner (Small Scale Industries) Ministry of Small Scale Industries (2000) "SSI in India the growth sector for the millennium" published by the development commissioner (SSIs) Ministry of SSIs and Agro and Rural Industries Government of India.
9. Punam Aggarwal and Vibha Mahajan (2003), "Challenges posed for SSIs by WTO", An Organization of Ministry of SSI Government of India, NISIET Hyderabad. 34-38.
10. Godbole, M.D. (1978), Industrial Dispersal Policies, Himalya Publishing House, Bombay,
11. Hugget, Richard and Mayar (1981), Lain Geography: Theory in practice – Industry, Harper and Row Publishers, London, 85.
12. Dadibhavi R.V. and Bagalkoti S.T. (2006), "Reforms and Regional Inequalities in India, an Analysis".

CHAPTER 2

Impact of World Trade Organisation and its Rules and Regulations

Abstract

This study particularly aims at the analysis and exploration of the influence of the policy change took place in the country, with the adoption of the resolution of WTO. The roots of WTO may be traced back to 1st January 1948 on which the General Agreement on Tariffs and Trade (GATT) came in to force. The UN Economic and Social Council came to be constituted to draft the charter for a propose International Trade Organization by the original 23 countries. Since the charter was not ratified. Hence the General Agreement remained the only International Instrument laying down trade rules. In December 1993, there were 111 contracting parties and a further 22 countries applying GATT resolution on a defects basis on 15th April 1994, Trade Ministers of 123 countries signed the final Act of the GATT. On 1st January 1995 the Uruguay Round of Negotiations at Marakesh formed WTO. Presently the WTO has 150-member countries.

The object of the Act is the liberalization of World Trade, the member countries were agreed to adopt fair Trade rules covering Commodities Services and Intellectual Property Rights. It provides for the lowering of tariffs on industrial goods and tropical products. The abolition of import duties on a variety of items and progressive abolition of quotas on textiles and garments, gradual reduction of trade distorting subsidies and import barriers and agreement on Intellectual Property and Trade in Service. The member countries were required to accept the resolution of the urgency round talks in their entirety and subscribe to all the WTO agreement and displines. There is no enforcement procedure. However decisions are ultimately reached by consensus. The WTO is the legal and institutional foundation of the Multinational Trading Systems. The trade policy review mechanism was accepted in 1994. It was broaden in 1995. It has been observed by Professor Raju in his Article "The recent environmental changes and impact on Small Scale Industrial Sector" that the policy framework (in the direction of LPG) instead of strengthening the economic structure will produce bizarre consequences like triggering uncontrolled chain reaction in which the weakened defense less sector like the SSI is most likely to suffer .This paper attempts to- 1. The general implications of resolutions and policy settlement of WTO 2. It was contemplated by certain countries that a global international organization dealing with the rules of regulations of trade between member nation 3. The Impact of LPG on Small Scale Industries

Introduction

This study particularly aims at the analysis and exploration of the influence of the policy change took place in the country, with the adoption of the resolution of WTO. The roots of WTO may be traced back to 1st January 1948 on which the General Agreement on Tariffs and trade (GATT) came in to force. The UN economic and social council came to be constituted to draft the charter for a propose International Trade Organization by the original 23 countries. Since the charter was not ratified. Hence the General Agreement remained the only International Instrument laying down Trade rules. In December 1993 there were 111 contracting parties and a further 22 countries applying GATT resolution on a defects basis on 15th April 1994, Trade Ministers of 123 countries signed the final Act of the GATT. On 1st January 1995 the Uruguay Round of Negotiations at Marakesh formed WTO. Presently the WTO has 150-member countries.

The object of the Act is the liberalization of World Trade the member countries were agreed to adopt fair trade rules covering Commodities Services and Intellectual Property Rights. It provides for the lowering of tariffs on industrial goods and tropical products. The abolition of import duties on a variety of items and progressive abolition of quotas on textiles and garments, gradual reduction of trade distorting subsidies and import barriers and agreement on Intellectual Property and Trade in Service. The member countries were required to accept the resolution of the urgency round talks in their entirety and subscribe to all the WTO agreement and displines. There is no enforcement procedure. However decisions are ultimately reached by consensus.

The WTO is the legal and institutional foundation of the Multinational Trading Systems. The trade policy review mechanism was accepted in 1994. It was broaden in 1995. All members are subject to review under TRPM, which mandates that 4 members with the largest share of world trade i.e. European Union, USA, Japan. The review period initially for every two years. After that the next sixteen every four years and others every six years with a longer period able to be fixed for the least developed members countries. The Trade Policies review body conducts the reviews. On the basis a policy statement by the member country under review and a report by economists in the secretariat trade policy review division. In case of any disputes between member countries, disputes settlement body was set up deal with appeals were permitted against the verdict of disputes settlement body an appellate body comprised of 97 members was also constituted. The verdict of the appellate body was binding on both the parties. The previous GATT secretariat was made to serve the WTO. WTO has no resources of its own other than its operating Budget. Head quarters of WTO its in Zenova – Switzerland[2]. (Source: Political thought year book 2007. The most updated FactFinder and quiz Builders, publication chrofricle books, Division of chronicle, New Delhi PP. 645 –651).

The WTO came in to existence on the basis of the theoretical agreements put forth by classical and Neo classical economist. It was argued that free trade would increase the efficiency and potentiality of production with best qualities of goods being produced for the masses. Therefore it was contemplated by certain countries that a global international organization dealing with the rules and regulations of trade between member nation, ultimately led to the set up of WTO[1] (Jaya- Krishna -2004). The major objectives put forth for the establishment of WTO are to secure full employment, raising standard of living, optimum use of the world's resources, increasing production and trade to increase the income of member countries. The core of WTO is in its framework agreements and negotiations, which are signed and legally approved by the 145 member countries in the year

2004. The main objective behind these agreements and negotiations is to support products of goods and services, intellectual property rights, export and import.

Historically speaking the base of the WTO lies in the GATT. Therefore the WTO is the successor to GATT. It is rapidly establishing itself as the 3rd of pillars of the Britton Woods Institutions along with IMF and IBRD.Which has come into existence in 1944 itself. India itself is one of the 23 founder members of these institutions.

WTO has underlined six fundamentals namely - Club of Nations, Free trade among countries, Non restrictive trade with some exception. Tariffs based on bound rates after negotiations. Dismantling of Non Tariff Barriers and all countries to be accorded, Most Favored Nations Status. In short it is a regulatory body of the world trade to ensure free transparent and predictable trading regimes in the world. WTO monitors compliance by member countries with number of agreements, which collectively governs multiple dimensions of trade relationship among member countries. It also acts as a disputes settlement body between member countries. Therefore all the member countries are bound to respect their commitments to different trade agreements under WTO.

The general implications of resolutions and policy settlement of WTO can be summarized as fallows.

1. The impact of the WTO and its agreements of an every economic activities- agriculture, trade, service, manufacturing etc.
2. The lowering of tariffs had dismantling of other restriction in developed and developing countries opened the world markets to enlightened and awakened entrepreneurs for greater opportunities.
3. Lowering of tariffs opened the domestic markets for free entry of foreign goods and foreign companies to set up their industrial units locally. This is increasingly threatened the domestic.
4. Whereas the developing countries have greater opportunities in sectors in which they have cost based advantages i.e. textiles, agriculture etc, the developed country will benefit by opening of service sector and tightening of intellectual

property rights. However with out corresponding reforms in their domestic economic reforms in their domestic economic policies developing countries may fail to benefit from WTO.

5. Export market will became together because of competition among developing countries having similar comparative advantages.
6. There is a way of standardization growing across the globe products from developing countries are to face tougher quality standard in developed markets. Particularly in the areas where they have comparative cost advantage.
7. Every company whether serving domestic or international market will have to undertake internal exercise to identify factors affecting its international competitiveness in terms of cost as well as quality. It will importable or tariff are further lowered or both.
8. The WTO will benefit those countries more, which exhibit wits and wisdoms and skill in the on going dialogue. The governments that are in constant tough with their industries and affected groups will be able to determine with the best of these advantages.
9. The International Trade is increasingly becoming knowledge based on entrepreneurial ability will come to force in the new environment[4].

The above features of WTO clearly indicate even though without making use of the words LPG. It has brought in all these three aspects in to the governance of the economies of its member countries.

The policy of liberalization is an extension of the policy initiated in 1985 itself. Therefore the NEP announcement of July 1991 is just an extension. The silent features of the policy of liberalization are-:

1. Opening up of the economy to the private sectors in the areas higher to reserve for the public sector.
2. Facilitating foreign investment and import of foreign technology
3. Abolition of the ceiling on assets for MRTP companies. Thus facilitating the expansions of MRTP companies and dominant undertakings.

4. Review the policy with respect to public sector undertakings :

   a) Limiting the Public sector strategic and essential infrastructure. Referring sick PSUS to board of industrial and financial reconstructions.
   b) This investing a part of the share holding of the public sector units.
   c) Granting greater autonomy for public sector units through the instrument of memorandum of understanding.
   d) To develop a safety net for workers who are like to be retreated as a result of measures to close down sick unit are rationalization of the staffing pattern of PSUs.

In short liberalization is nothing but a policy of providing a free and unrestricted policy framework for the Industrial undertakings of WTO member countries for the inflow and out flow of all the resources – Men and Means along with the finished and unfinished goods between themselves. More simply a movement launched by WTO towards the free trade without any sort of barriers.

Privatization is a concept originated from the philosophy of liberalization. As a result of perusing the policy of liberalization free movement of goods and services between markets ultimately lead to the survival of the fittest. Therefore the units producing the goods and commodities including services. Which enjoys least cost advantages will survive in the market. Others become sick and ultimately go out of market. i.e. closure. In order to avoid such situations the governments concerned have to modify the policies in case of their own industrial units. i.e. public understandings. The modification is just handing over such units manufacturing or service units to private entrepreneurs. In addition to such things private investments given a total freedom to in which sector the investor is interested. This ultimately provides for the dominance of private sector.

Globalization is more a romantic world indicating the desired to integrate nations - stages within the overall framework of the WTO. It is more a modern versions of the theory of "comparative cost advantages" propagated by classical economists. It is a strong theoretical ground provided by the classicalists for the unrestricted flow goods between countries. The theory of comparative cost advantage fundamentally was framed at the time of colonial administration. It provided a strong ground for Great Briton to move their goods to other less developed countries. In the present era it has came in a new version. I.e. Globalization. It is noting but opening of the domestic market to the international or global market of all the WTO member countries.

The policy of LPG is nothing but providing freedom to the total markets of WTO member countries from the licenses, inspectorates and burocratism. Under measures gradual removing of all these impediments on the way of the free movement of investment goods and services between markets of WTO members.

In the successive pages let us investigate how these policy measures have influence the small scale industrial sector of the Indian economy.

The Impact of LPG on Small Scale Industries

From the days of GATT till the birth of WTO on 1st January 1995. after several agreements and negotiations, and several rounds of talks between the founder countries several policy statements were framed to govern the bilateral and multilateral trade with regard to all aspects. India being one of the 23 founders members of WTO by 30th March 2005 completed about 10 years. During this period the economy to go on the footstep of member countries underwent many changes. As and when the policy statements, rules and regulation changed. By a review of literature on the changes occurred in the economy during this period exhibits a sort of controversial aspects. Though we are not concerned with all such controversial aspects, it is necessity here to take into consideration the observations made by few authors. Particularly with reference to industrial sectors that too with a special reference to SSI sector. It is glaring to note here that some opinions are infavour of the influences. Where as some are contradictory. Let us have a bird's eye view on this controversy in the successive lines.

Though we are concerned with the particular study of its impact on SSIs, we have to remember that the policy literature on general impact of WTO and its agreements on SSI's are not different from its implications on industry, are whole because they comprise the major part of the Indian Industrial sector. (Because the SSIs of the country contribute about 54% of the Non – traditional and 10% of the traditional product exports (Taken together about 35% of total exports of our country). Further we have to accept that extensive information's on WTO is visible but these studies, which associated with SSI's in particular with regard to the Indian economy, are very few. Even the scope of the studies made here to with particular reference to SSIs.

Let us observe the comments made by leading authorities on the impact of WTO on SSIs:

Jain observed- "by the inevitable by the Globalization the SSI sector was some what over protected. The hope that the infant would grow into an adult who could be freed to face competition has been completely believed. The SSIs never had a strong desired to grow to medium and large scale because of the benefits of protection given to it. Many of the policies also discouraged the growth of SSIs units into large one and had a stunting effect on manufacturing, employment and output growth. With Globalization they are more exposed to severe competition both from large-scale sector, domestic and foreign, and from the MNCs.

A few research organizations and industrial association have assessed the impact of ERs and policy changes on the SSI sector. The highlights of sum of the studies carried out in the post liberalization period are summarized here-

The national council of Applied Research and Fridrich Neumann stifttung (**NCRER-FNST**) conducted a detailed study on structure and promotion of SSIs in India. The report was finalized in December 1993. This report, the findings of the study (Source: SIDB Annual Report, 1999) are with reference to-

1. The product range quantum of value addition, capital utilization and employment, the SSI sector is highly non-homogeneous.
2. Compare to non-tiny enterprises in the field of investment, technology, management, market products, wages etc tiny units exhibits different characteristics.
3. Poor quality of production, technology and quality control

is another factor the productive activity is carried in the use of more than 56.6 percent of manual power.

The report in the light of its observation concluded the future of SSIs could be bright provided steps were taken to enable SSI units to be competitive and innovative. Further it insisted on the need for infrastructure facilities and inputs to SSI sector. National Institute of Public Finance and Policy **(NIPEP)** conducted a quick field study during 1994-95 covering 300 SSI units of five states and two union territories during 1994-95.This survey aimed at assessing the impact of budgetary changes in the central excise policy with regard to the SSI sector. The study indicated an adverse impact of the withdrawal of excise concession on the products of manufactured by SSI units. As a result many units have diversified or even closed down their activities. Another study made by this institute on central fiscal incentives and concessions to SSIs impact on growth and structure **(NIPFP)** pointed out certain important aspects. They are:

1. Particularly SSI has responded very well export incentives after 1991. As a result their share in the total export of country went up.
2. Advanced technology came to be incorporated in the place of human labour.
3. Capital productivity as well labour productivity went up indicating a potential growth.
4. Due to increase in the size of employment capital and output particularly in case of units producing unreserved items their performance came to be better.
5. Due to concessional finance by banks has been observed as most important incentives for all size groups of SSIs.

The study reveals that in the face of competition from larger enterprises, SSIs suffer from many handicaps. Such as inadequate and irregular supply of raw materials access to appropriate technology, shortage of working capital and marketing facilities. However, the study observes any support beyond a limit is irrational and unjustified. Another important survey conducted in the year 1996 by **CII** revealed certain important aspects. The main findings for the study were[13]

1. 40 percent of respondents had increased their

competitiveness in terms of quality of their product, packaging, efficiency etc in the post liberalization period.

2. 21 percent of responding units had found an increase in export orders and 37 percent increase their product range.
3. 24 percent of respondents units faced increased competition in their product categories and
4. 33 percent of their respondents felt an increased in their cost of production.

Further the business outlook survey on small industry by CII 1996 NCAER study conducted in 1996-97 again the business outlook survey on small industry by CII 1998 have observed that due to the policy changes. The SSI sector suffered with many adverse influences and exposed to severe competition. The survey of CII 1998 particularly observed the lack of credit and finance, shortage of power and other infrastructure facilities, inadequate marketing facilities and shortage of raw materials have put the SSI sector in to a deteriorating condition. It has been observed by Professor Raju in his Article "The recent environmental changes and impact on Small Scale Industrial Sector" that the policy framework (in the direction of LPG) instead of strengthening the economic structure will produce bizarre consequences like triggering uncontrolled chain reaction in which the weakened defense less sector like the SSI is most likely to suffer.

Two distinctive implications are possible to be observed due to the WTO policies and agreements on the SSI sector of the country. As such SSI's have availed some opportunities and also they have to face threats wooing to WTO and its agreements. As observed the main opportunities of the WTO are bought fewer than three heads – Firstly national treatment (or MFN) for exportable items across the countries all over the World with better market access through internet. Secondly enlightened entrepreneurs have greater opportunities to benefit from their comparative advantages due to lowering of tariffs and dismantling of other impediments. Finally the industries that are in constant touch in government, which inturn negotiates the best of their interest in the on going dialogue with WTO are going to benefit.

In contrast to the above observations the SSIs are exposed

for serious threats – SSI's have to face severe competition by way of cheap imports from different countries due to the removal of quantitative restrictions of exports and slashing down of tariffs. Due to this every single individual enterprise whether small or big, whether exporting or the domestic market has to face serious competition. In addition OGL opens of the possibility of direct competition in the domestic market in the imports of high quality goods from developed countries and cheap products from other less developed countries. Subsequently entry of multinational companies in the different fields of production into the economy intensified the competition in the domestic markets. As a result the sector is not in a position to face the competition due to its inbuilt weakness like poor quality, costly and difficult credit, weak and non-available infrastructure, traditional technology, outdated mechanical structure, inflexible labour laws, lack of international exposer and ineffective association. Further export market will become very tough because of competition among developing countries with similar comparative cost advantages. There would be bigger threats of dumping by developed countries, which push the SSIs of developing countries into hot waters.

Many legislations, rules and regulations, and amendments have been made by the union as well state governments concerned the economic activity of the country in its all directions. These legislations laws etc have affected directly and also indirectly, the SSI units of the state. One such may be pointed out as an example for this- The recent legislation and amendment with regard to agricultural produces marketing corporation provides a free scope for entry of foreign investment into this sector. On its face it looks an Act concerning the produces of agricultural marketing. But this ultimately leads to entry of foreign companies into the field of marketing of agricultural product. In the first instance affecting all the APMCs activities, later the retailers. And other labour force involved. At the second stage it allow for contract farming – large-scale holdings, large-scale farming, mechanization of agriculture, displacement of small-scale holders etc. Ultimately affect the delivery of raw materials to SSIs depending upon agricultural sector. There by indirectly put the SSIs of the country to hardships.

Growth Pattern of Small Scale Industries in India

SSIs units in out study period exhibit a steady growth. In all direction before the adoption of new ERs. This is clear in the table given below for the period 1977-78 to 1990-91.

Year	*Units (Lakh Nos.)*	*Rate of Growth*	*At 1993-94 Prices*	*Rate of Growth*	*At current Prices*	*Rate of Growth*	*Employment (Lakh No,)*	*Rate of Growth*	*Export (Rs. crores)*	*Rate of Growth*
1977-78	0.8	0	6000	0	1900	0	4.2	0.00	100	0
1978-79	0.60	-25.00	5400	-10.00	1500	-21.05	9.8	-90.20	300	200.00
1979-80	0.80	33.33	8200	51.85	5800	286.67	3.2	-96.80	100	-66.67
1980-81	0.60	-25.00	5800	-29.27	6500	12.07	4	-96.00	400	300.00
1981-82	0.90	50.00	6100	5.17	4500	-30.77	4	-96.00	500	25.00
1982-83	1.00	11.11	6400	4.92	2400	-46.67	4	-96.00	-100	-120.00
1983-84	1.00	0.00	8800	37.50	6600	175.00	5.2	-94.80	200	-300.00
1984-85	0.80	-20.00	11100	26.14	8900	34.85	5.8	-94.20	300	50.00
1985-86	1.10	37.50	13500	21.62	10700	20.22	6	-94.00	300	0.00
1986-87	1.10	0.00	15500	14.81	11100	3.74	5.4	-94.60	800	166.67
1987-88	1.20	9.09	16900	9.03	15000	35.14	5.6	-94.40	800	0.00
1988-89	1.30	8.33	19400	14.79	19100	27.33	6	-94.00	1100	37.50
1989-90	1.10	-15.38	20000	3.09	25900	35.60	6.6	-93.40	2100	90.91
1990-91	49.70	4418.18	-105172	-625.86	-53498	-306.56	38.7	-61.30	2064	-1.71
Total	**62.00**	**4482.17**	**37928**	**-476.21**	**66402**	**225.57**	**108.5**	**-1195.70**	**8964**	**381.70**
AAG		**32015.50**		**-3401.50**		**1611.21**		**-8540.71**		**2726.43**

Source: Reserve Bank of India, Annual Report 2005-06, Bombay P-79.

Growth Pattern of Small Scale Industries in India
(Table given below for the period 1991-92 to 2004-05, After ERs)

Year	*Units (Lakh Nos.)*	*Rate of Growth*	*At 1993-94 Prices*	*Rate of Growth*	*At current Prices*	*Rate of Growth*	*Employment (Lakh No,)*	*Rate of Growth*	*Export (Rs. crores)*	*Rate of Growth*
1991-92	2.7	0	2627	0	1813	0	7.7	0	4219	0
1992-93	2.9	7.41	4891	86.18	3798	109.49	8.8	14.29	3901	-7.54
1993-94	3	3.45	6550	33.92	14383	278.70	7.8	-11.36	4220	8.18
1994-95	3.1	3.33	9978	52.34	23358	62.40	8.8	12.82	3761	-10.88
1995-96	3.2	3.23	12401	24.28	25558	9.42	6.5	-26.14	4221	12.23
1996-97	3.4	6.25	13717	10.61	20093	-21.38	8	23.08	2778	-34.19
1997-98	3.5	2.94	11371	-17.10	19412	-3.39	7.3	-8.75	4222	51.98
1998-99	3.7	5.71	11262	-0.96	23237	19.70	7.4	1.37	4537	7.46
1999-00	3.8	2.70	12854	14.14	23306	0.30	8.5	14.86	4223	-6.92
2000-01	3.9	2.63	14022	9.09	27537	18.15	9.6	12.94	15597	269.33
2001-02	4.1	5.13	11212	-20.04	20973	-23.84		-100.00	4224	-72.92
2002-03	4.3	4.88	15023	33.99	29723	41.72	10.9	10.90	14769	249.64
2003-04	4.5	4.65	18094	20.44	45740	53.89	11.2	2.75	4225	-71.39
2004-05	4.6	2.22	22781	25.90	60530	32.33	11.2	0.00	-97644.00	-2411.10
Total	**50.7**	**54.53**	**166783.00**	**272.79**	**339461.00**	**577.49**	**113.70**	**-53.24**	**-22747.00**	**-2016.10**
AAG		**389.50**		**1948.50**		**4124.93**		**-380.29**		**-14400.71**

Source: Reserve Bank of India Annual Report 2005-06 Bombay P. 79

Before ERs

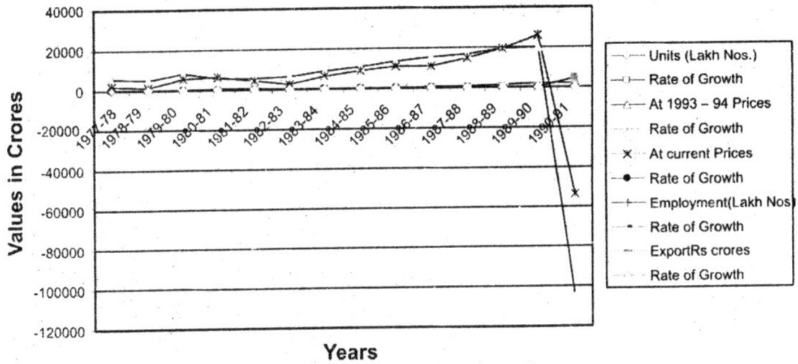

After ERs

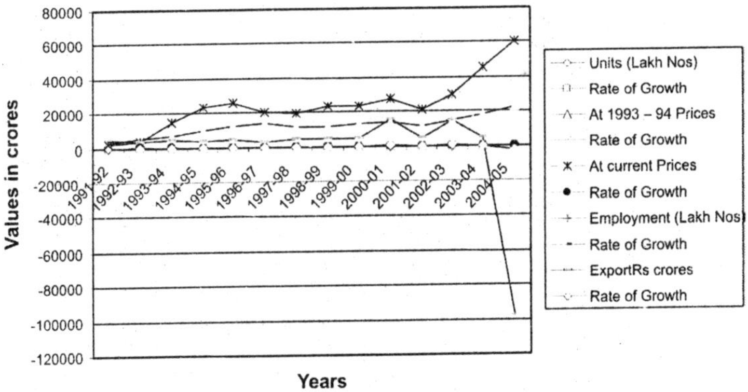

The number units working 1977-78 were Rs. 0.8 lakhs. It went up to Rs. 49.70 lakhs in the year 1990-91. Out of the total number of units Rs. 62.00 lakhs in the country particularly in the year 1990-91 there is a small formidable growth in the small scale units. This is mainly due to the policy changes that took place in the country. Particularly with regard to SSIs in the year 1988-89 and 1990-91.

However, it is positive in the rate of growth both at 1993-94 prices and at current prices also the rate of growth is non-positive.

The SSIs in the country have provided employment to a large number of people. In the year 1977-78 it employed this sector provided employment to Rs. 4.2 lakhs in the year 1978-79 the employment provided SSI units went up to Rs. 9.8 lakhs . However, till 1989-90 it indicates the employment does not increase to two digits. But in the year 1990-91 the employment provided by the sector all of a sudden went up ro Rs. 38.70 lakhs out of Rs. 108.50 lakhs. This is due to fiscal expansion we have noticed in the number of units came into existence in the particular period.

In case of exports the SSI units have registered a grater increase in exports in the year 1989-90 to the extent of Rs. 2100 crores. However, there is a fall to the extent of 1.71 percent.

When the ERs (Economic Reforms 1991-92to 2004-05) came into operation i.e., from 1991-92 to 2004-05 the changes occurred with regard to different aspects of SSIs is not so much encouraging. Though it appears to be positive it is negligible. The number of units in the year 1991-92 the number units came into existence was 2.7 lakhs units. The number of units though increases for all the years by 2004-05 the number went up to 4.6 lakhs that rising the total number units 50.70 lakhs in the whole country during the period 1991-92 to 2004-05. Even here in the previous period it is not so much encouraging in case of employment during this period it has provided employment to 113.70 laksh persons. In the year 2004-05 and for the proceeding year the volume of employment remained stagnant. For other years i.e., from 1991-92 to 2002-03 the increase is not encouraging. In case of exports leaving during which the value of exports Rs. 15597 crores and in the year 2002-03 during which it was Rs. 14769 crores. But in all the other years the changes took place is very less and in certain years it is not positive. This totally indicates after the ERs came to be adopted this sector has not shown an encouraging performance.

Conclusion

The comparative pictures of the above data as show that the industrial policies evolved by the Government of India put the whole SSI sector in to a hot water. This is purely because of the policy of the Liberalization and Globalization put to operation indiscrimately. In order to bring about even distribution of SSI's in different regions of the country, to encourage and help prospective persons to establish SSIs in the backward areas, The only way to liberate the SSI in the country is to evolve a policy of easy credit, marketing, Tax free period, Reservation of products for manufacturing, De-licensing, Lessening of bueracrating control, upgradition of technology etc

Reference

1. Jeevan Reddy B.P.(2002), " Patents and Trade Marks: Impact on Small Scale and Medium Scale Industries", sedme, Vol. 29(1), NISIET Hyderabad: 1-3.
2. GATT (1991), "Trade Policy Review Mechanism, European Communities, March, Geneva: GATT
3. Jaya Krishna (2004), World Trade Origination and its Implications on Small Scale Industries in Karnataka' Sedme, Vol.31 (2) June, NISIET Hyderabad: 91.
4. Syed Vazith Hussain (2003), 'SSIs in the New Millennium", Sarup and Sons New Delhi; 144-161.
5. Dr. Gad wale H.H. (2004), "Impact of Liberalization Policy on Industrial Relations in India", Southern Economist Journal Val (43(2); 5-8.
6. Brij Bhushan (1997), "SSIs in the New era of Economic Liberalization: Challenges and Priorities for the Ninth Plan", Kurukshetra Vol.XLV (8), New Delhi; 44-48.
7. Dr.Gopal Krishna V.S.(2005), " Impact of WTO on SMEs" Quest Publications Mumbai. 18-19.
8. Neelam Jain (2004), "Small Scale Industries in the New Millennium" Journal of Sedme, Volume-32 (3), NISIET Hyderabad 64-72).
9. SIDBI (1999), "Policy Impact – Key Findings Small Scale Industries Sector Annual Report of 1999, SIDBI, Luck now, 151.
10. CII, NCAER (1996), "Impact of Policy initiatives, Policy Impact – Key findings of Various Studies, The Views of Small Industries and Gange its Perception of the impact of liberalization", SIDBI Annual Report 1999, SIDBI Luck now, 152-153.

CHAPTER 3

Necessary Finance for Small Scale Industries in India

One of the important problems of SSIs is the financial problem. The financial disability is beyond question. The internal resources of SSIs are so small that they have no surplus to leave on, during the period of business strain. This brings about out instability of their profit, which makes the banks apathetic towards extending loans to SSIs. For modern SSIs finance is very important and the financial requirement of SSIs can be conveniently classified into three types and they are venues capital long-term loans and short-term loans. The first one is of fundamental importance for establishing SSIs and the entrepreneurs themselves should provide it. Long-term capital is required for the acquisition of land for the construction of factory, building, acquiring machinery and equipment and other needed fixed assets. Short term capital necessary for meeting day to day expenditure such as purchase of raw materials, payment of daily wages, transportation charges, repairing of machinery, marketing expenditure, holding of stock of final products etc.,

The SSIs being financially weak. They have to depend upon different external sources available. Broadly the external sources of finance may be put here in a tabular form as next page.

The major portion of credit flows from these institutions involved in this direction, on the basis of the recommendations of different working groups and committees constituted by RBI and the government. A birds-eye view is given in the following lines.

Policy Measures for Financing SSIs

Recognizing the very important role played by Small Scale Industries(SSIs) in the industrial economy of the country, the total

Table 1: Institutional Network for Providing Non-Financial Assistance Institutional network for financing SSIs

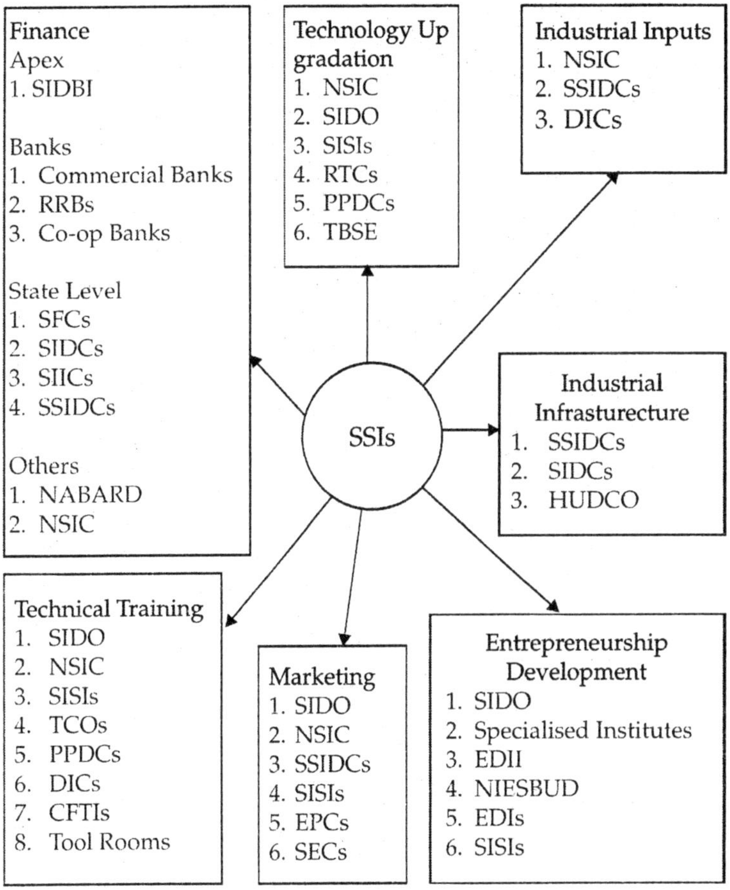

Source: National Small Industries Corporation, Annual Report of 2006-07

amount of financial assistance extended to SSIs constitutes a very small part of the total amount of the financial assistance extended to industries nevertheless there is still a need for a positive change in the outlook and approach of commercial banks and development banks towards SSIs.The credit worthiness of SSIs should not be judged in terms of the value of the assets but in terms of the capacity of the SSIs to do the business and earn profit.

This calls for the evolution of a system of integrated financial assistance where by long term and short term loans are extended in required amount at a reasonable interest rate. The financial and non-financial problems of SSIs have to be attended to simultaneously for healthy growth of SSIs .For this purpose an elaborate system of financial assistance has been evolved by the union government and States Governments in India. Now there are specialized financial institutions for catering into the financial needs of SSIs as is done in Germany.

The first step in the direction of funding SSIs was under the State Aid to Industries Act. The next important step in this direction was the passing of the State Financial Corporations Act in 1951 for making provisions for the State Governments for setting up of State Financial Corporations with the purpose of extending medium and long term loans to medium and small scale industries. The State Bank of India and its allied banks have evolved special schemes of financial assistance for meeting the financial needs of SSIs. The RBI evolved a Credit Guarantee Scheme for SSIs in 1960. The Central Bank takes upon itself the role of Credit-Guarantee Organizations for the advances, which are left unpaid including interest overdue and recoverable charges. This includes long-term loans also the National Small Industries Corporations introduce a Credit Guarantee Scheme (1966), to ensure cent percent financial assistance to SSIs. The introduction of the social control on commercial banks by the union finance ministry (1967) was another milestone to activate commercial banks in extending financial assistance to SSIs in an active manner. The nationalization of 14 nationalized commercial banks 1969, and six more commercial banks 1980 ushered in a new area of funding SSIs in the Indian Economy.

In 1980 the central bank issued certain directives to commercial banks pertaining to priority sector lending and expected their co-operation and compliance. According to the RBI, priority sector advances should form 40% of aggregate bank credit. Commercial Bank credit to rural artisans, village craftsmen and cottage industries should be at least being 12.5 % of the total advances to SSIs.

The refinance assistance scheme introduced by the Apex finance institution to SSIs i.e., Industrial Development Bank of India together with the Credit Guarantee Scheme created a very favorable atmosphere for the flow of credit assistance to SSIs. In May 1988, IDBI created the small industries development fund, this was popularly known as SIDF. The main objective of SIDF was to speed up the flow of credit assistance to SSIs and to provide a focal point to coordinate at the apex level. The availability of both financial and non-financial assistance from different SSIs production institution for proper growth of SSIs in the country. Government of India in August 1997 introduced National Equity Fund Scheme, this popularly known as NEF Scheme, with the main objective of extending helping hand in the form of equity assistance to SSIs. Another important addition in the field of evolution of financial policy, setting up of an exclusive financial institution at the national level was the small industrial Development Bank of India (SIDBI). SIDBI administered SIDF, NEF and other schemes of financial assistance for SSIs which were earlier administered by IDBI. The RBI took another important measure to review the flow of industrial finance to SSIs and to suggest measures for improving the performance of the delivery system in security of adequate financial assistance to the SSIs.

To mention a few, some committees were constituted and their recommendations here appear to be important. In the year 1991 the Nayak Committee came to be constituted by RBI. This committee went through different aspect of adequacy of credit that was being advanced to the SSI sector and also the time involved in processing loan applications of SSIs. This committee found that the SSI sector was receiving advances only to the extent of 8.1 percent of their annual output, which was below the normative requirement of 20%. On the basis of the recommendation made by the committee the RBI advised banks to grant working capital to SSIs to the extent of 20% of their projected annual turnover. The Nayak committee took cognizes of delay involved in processing loan applications of SSIs for credit advised the RBI to take measures for the quick dispersal of credit, to SSIs. On the basis of this, RBI (Reserve Bank of India) also issued a number of circulars advising banks to process loan applications without delay. In addition taking into consideration the localization aspect of SSIs wherever the SSIs are centralized RBI asked to setup specialized bank branches. Primarily to serve the SSI units.

Later the recommendations of this committee were came to be incorporated in the seven-point action plan announced by the finance minister in his budget speech of 1995-96 to enhance the flow of credit to SSI sector. The recommendations came to be incorporated in the seven point action plan were – setting up of specialized SSI branches, delegation of powers to the branch and regional levels, conduct sample surveys of their performing SSI account to find out whether they were getting adequate credit to provide both term loan as well working capital to SSI entrepreneurs. Simplification of procedural formalities by banks for SSIs to have regular meetings both at zonal and regional level with the SSI entrepreneurs to know the problems particularly with reference to credit facilities and sensitization of bank managers towards working of SSI sector.

Another important committee, in this direction came to be appointed in the year 1997-98 under the chairmanship of S.L. Kapur RBI appointed one-man committee to study the credit delivery system to the SSI sector and suggest measure for improving delivery system and also simplifying the procedural formalities for credit to the SSI Sector. This committee submitted its report to RBI on 30th 1998. This committee report contained 126 specific recommendations to solve the problems of credit of SSI sector. The major recommendation of the committee is as follows:

- Special treatment to smaller among the small industries
- Enhancement in the limits of composite loan from Rs. 2 lakh to 5 lakhs.
- Simplification of procedural formalities raising exemption limit for equilateral security from Rs. 25,000 to Rs. 5 Lakhs.
- Enhancement of SIDBI's role and states to match with that of NABARD. Opening more specialized SSI bank branches. Allowing access to low cost funds to SIDBI for refinancing SSI loans. Setup of collateral reserve fund to provide to first party Guarantee. Introduction of credit Guarantee scheme.
- Further in the year 1999 – 2000 a several initiative step were taken in the budget. This budget allowed for the launching of Credit Insurance Scheme, enhancement of composite loan, and enhancement of working capital loan from Rs. 1 crore to Rs 5 crores on the basis of annual turnover.

- This study group constituted earlier that is S.P. Gupta Study group submitted its interim report in July 2000. It suggested several measures particularly with reference to financial aspects of SSIs. The most important once are setting up of targets for tiny & SSI units for credit from banks and financial institution under proprietary sector lending.
- Need for reduction in the cost of credit for SSIs. Setting up of more specialized branches for SSI sector. Standardization procedure and simplification of norms by banks, more effective monitoring of credit flow to SSI sector by the monitoring committee of RBI.
- Easy and reasonable cost credit to SSIs.
- Rising of the limit of composite loans from 10 lakhs to 25 lakhs to encourage tiny units. Not to cover all future fixed asset of assisted unit for securing its advances.
- Measures for time bound disposal of loan application and easy documentation.

Taking into consideration the recommendation of Nayak committee, Kapur Committee and Dr S.P. Gupta study group a comprehensive policy package was announced by the Government in August 2000.

The RBI from time to time took measures to improve the credit delivery system to SSI units. At large the RBI resorted to "Moral Suasion" to ensure the easy flow of finance to SSI sector. This includes opening up of specialized branches by public sectors banks, delegation of more powers to branch managers in extending credit facilities to SSI. Extension of single window scheme to all districts to provide financial needs of SSI etc., (Source FICCI, New Delhi)

Further to smoothen the flow of credit to SSI sector; the RBI and the Government took a number of measures (Same page 1 of 1 internet RBI). It initiated the credit information bureau of India Ltd., to workout solutions that would provide comprehensive credit reports. The RBI reviewing all its existing guidelines on financing SSI sector, debt restructuring, nursing of sick units etc., with an intension of rationalizing, consolidating and liberalizing, several guidelines were provided to the banking institutions. The Boards of Banks are advice to formulate more & more liberal and appropriate schemes for the easy flow of adequate credit to SSI sector. The RBI and the Government again found the necessity of finding the drawbacks in the easy flow of credit and adequate finance (Annexure research division) to SSI sector. It constituted a working committee under the chairmanship of A.S. J. Ganguly, Director, and central board of RBI in the year 2004.

In support of the policy measures recommended by the several working groups and advisory committees, the RBI and the Government from time to time framed several policy measures, directives and advises to the financial institutions engaging in financing SSI sector of the country. Let us here note down the financial institutions involved in providing financial assistance to SSI sector of the country. The institution wise status of credit deployment and the operational strategy for the SSI sector is summarized in the following lines.

The Small Industrial Development Bank of India came to be established as per the Act of parliament. It is an All India Principal Financial Institution for the promotion, financing and development of SSI sector. It commence it operation on April 2, 1990. The financial institutions of the country are directed to function in accordance and co-ordination with the SIDBI. SIDBI formulated several schemes for the easy and adequate flow of credit to SSI units of the country through several financial institutions. Further it also formulated schemes for the overall improvement of the SSI sectors. The present lending rate of SIDBI has been kept at 11-50 percent per annum. The SIDBI sanctioned credit up to 2004-05 Rs.103496 crores and dispersal Rs 69703 crores.

A major segment of the Indian financial system consists of commercial banks. They are the most important source of institution of credit in India. The commercial banks have launched a number of schemes for the promotion of SSI sector. Private as well foreign banks are also extending financial assistance to SSI sector. Commercial banks have extended credit to SSI sector. . Further the Regional Rural Banks and Co-operative Banks are also extending credit to SSI but it is not cognizable. However the tiny industries, cottage & small scale industries are the major aim of these the Rural Co-operative Banks.

State level Institutions

Under the institutional framework for credit dispersion state financial corporations play a cognizable rule in extending credit to SSI sector. Long term credit to small & medium scale industries are being provided with all facilities needed from time to time, State Finance Corporations introduce diversifications in their activities. The SFC of Karnataka as sanctioned Rs 333070.86 lakhs of rupees and dispersed 329935.70 lakhs of rupees(March 2005) to SSI sector under various schemes. The state Industrial Development Corporations and State Industrial Investment Corporations are also being established primarily to cater to the financial needs of medium & large such Industries. These institutions to here and there be financing the SSI sector.

Other Institutions

NABARD, Khadi and Village Industries Commission, NSICL, North Eastern Development Finance Corporation Ltd., are also financing tiny and small scale industrial units of the country.The Government of India and the RBI Independently sometimes jointly appointed a number of committees and working groups to recommend suitable measures to facilitate and promote the easy flow of credit to SSIs sector. To disseminate authentic information (SIDBI- 2001 page 109) and to checkup the authentically of information furnished by entrepreneurs and working group was appointed by the RBI under the chairmanship Sree N.H.Sidque. This group recommended several measures in this regard in november 1999.

Taking into consideration the most prominent development in international finance in recent times to pooling up and replacing of homogenous illiquid loans into marketable securities, an working group was constituted under the chairmanship U.S.N.Murthy which submitted its report in December 1999. On the basis of the recommendation ACT came into existence under the chairmanship of K.Madhavarao a high power committee on Urban Co-operative Banks (UCBs) came to be constituted to recommend necessary measures to reduce the systematic risks to financial system, to protect the depositors and to strengthen the UCBs.

Another major step was taken to facilitate the equilateral free/third party free, credit facilities to SSIs. The government of India in association with SIDBI launched the Credit Guarantee

Fund scheme for small industries from August1, 2000. In recent years the Honorable Prime Minister announced the ceiling on loans and advances to be covered under the scheme has been enhanced from Rs one million to Rs 2.5 million extended by banks. Selected Regional Rural Banks and such other institutions were directed to put this scheme into operation. On 31st August 2000 the Honorable Prime Minister launched another major scheme for the promotion of SSI Sector in the country. SSI Units engaged in manufacturing of several products were brought under this scheme .This scheme being implemented through SIDBI providing capital subsidy of 12 percent on loans and advances to SSI Units by schedule commercial banks and NSICL. Later extended to SFCs also. The scheme came to be named as credit linked capital scheme for technology and up-gradation of SSI.

To facilitate promotion and development of knowledge based enterprises primarily in the small and medium sector on March11, 2000 SIDBI announced a new programme under the caption SIDBI National Programme on Innovation and Incubation for SSIs. In addition to the above technology up-gradation fund scheme for textile and jute industries and Tannery Modernization Scheme too were launched. Particularly during Ninth and Tenth five year plans a number of recommendations were made by working groups in order to find the financial requirement of SSI Sector particularly term finance and working capital funds required by SSIs and to recommend measures to meet the needs of this sector.

Industrial Development Bank of India

The IDBI was established on July 1, 1964 under an Act of parliament as the principle financial institution for industrial development in the country. Later IDBI's ownership was transfer to Government of India in Feb 1976 consequent upon amendment of IDBI Act in 1995 to provide it with greater operational flexibility government reduce its holding to around 72% by opening shares of IDBI to the public for the first time. It caters to the growing and diverse needs of medium and large scale industries with the main objective of providing financial assistance and co-ordinating the working institutions engaged in financing, promoting and developing industries.

At the time of moving the said Act the Union Finance Minister addressing the parliament put the aims and goals , the IDBI – "that we are envisaging the new Industrial Development Bank of India as Central Co-ordinating agency which ultimately will be concerned directly or indirectly with all the problems or questions relating to the long and medium term financing of industries and will be in a position if necessary to adopt and enforce a system of Proprietary in promoting future industrial growth". IDBI provides different forms of financial assistance for the industrial growth of the country. Project finance, Equipment finance, Asset credit, Corporate loan, Working capital loan, Direct discounting bills, Equipment lease, Refinance for medium scale industries and Bills rediscounting at different rates of interest and also for different periods of terms.

With the establishment of SIDBI, the IDBI was inducted as one of the directors of the SIDBI. Since then SIDBI came out as a specialized institution for financing the SSI sector. However the IDBI since its inspection recognizing the importance of the development of SSI sector provided liberal financial assistance to SSI sector of the country. This is more clear in the table given below since its inception table. 2

Table 2: IDBI – Refinance Assistance to Small Scale Sector of Karnataka

Year(s)	*Total sanctions for small scale sectors of the country*	*Total disbursements for small scale sectors of the country*	*Rs. in crores of which for small scale sector of Karnataka*	
			Sanctions (%)	*Disbursements (%)*
1977-78	115.2	99.4	113 (9.81)	11.3 (11.37)
1978-79	273.8	196.9	15.0 (5.48)	15.9 (8.08)
1979-80	369.2	310.3	28.4 (7.69)	27.2 (8.77)
1980-81	417.6	344.0	23.8 (5.70)	25.3 (7.35)
1981-82	516.3	414.5	31.1 (6.02)	24.0 (5.79)
1982-83	688.2	545.9	50.3 (7.31)	40.1 (7.35)
1983-84	615.0	636.5	55.4 (9.01)	51.0 (8.01)
1984-85	882.97	727.11	92.9 (10.52)	69.1 (9.50)
1985-86	1132.70	795.12	105.4 (9.31)	80.4 (10.11)
1986-87	1239.49	985.54	108.3 (8.74)	90.9 (9.22)

1987-88	1498.54	1074.23	99.1 (6.61)	92.7 (8.63)
1988-89	1925.72	1319.18	115.6 (6.00)	89.3 (6.77)
1989-90	1255.23	1195.92	116.7 (9.30)	92.4 (7.73)

Source: IDBI- Report on development banking in India, 1977-78, 1980-81, 1984-85, 1988-89, 1989-90, Bombay: IDBI, pp 99,105,88,103,69.

Note: Refinance assistance includes assistance sanctioned and disbursed to small scale industries and small road transport operators under refinance and bills rediscounting schemes.

Graph : 1 IDBI – Refinance Assistance to Small Scale Sector of Karnataka

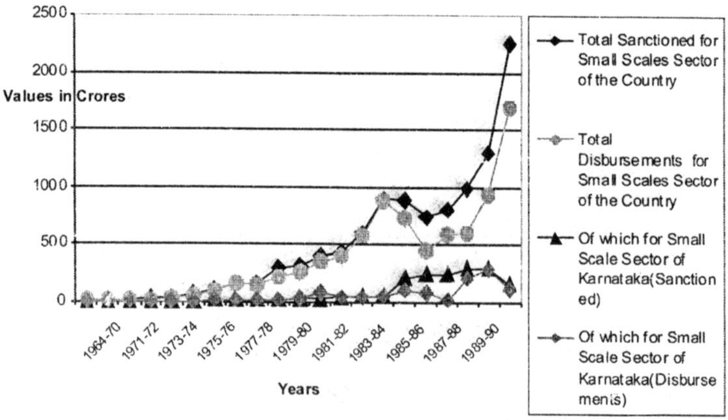

Being our study is limited to Karnataka since 1977 – 78 to 2004 – 05: the role of IDBI with regard to SSI sector is pointed out here as 1977 – 78 to 1989- 90. The successive period is covered by the SIDBI. In the year 1977 -78 the IDBI sanctioned 150.9 crores of rupees to SSI sector out of which Rs.146.2 crores was disbursed in the country. Out of this amount Karnataka's share is only 11.3 crores of rupees. Out of which Rs. 11 crores has been disbursed. Since 1977-78 throughout till 1988-89 there was an increasing trend. In the year 1988-89 the total amount sanctions to SSIs stood at 289.57 crores of rupees and the amount disbursed was 282.75 crores of rupees. But in the year 1989- 90 the amount sanction was 151.70 crores and 121.12 crores of rupees was disbursed. This appears leaving 1989- 90 the SSI Sector of Karnataka had a favorable treatment at the hands of IDBI.

Small Industies Development Bank of India (SIDBI)

Another major Institution, which is playing a dominating role. However after the Economic Reforms have been put to operation in the Country in encouraging SSI Sector is SIDBI. It came in to existence in April 1990 under Act of Indian parliament as the Principal Financial Institution for Promotion, Financing, Development of Industries in the SSIs and also coordinating functions of other Institutions engaged in similar activities. This institution provides financial assistance to SSIs in three ways i.e., a) Indirect Assistance to primarily Lending Institutions. b) Direct Assistance to Small Units. c) Development and Support Services.

The Indirect assistance of SIDBI to SSIs through a large network of 913 primary lending institutions spread over ,the country with a branch network of over 65000. For all administrative purposes the whole country is divided into Five Region as- Eastern region, North East region, Northern region, Western region, and South region The assistance is provided by way of refinance, bills rediscounting and resource supporting in the form of short term loans, line of credit in lieu of refinance etc. Direct assistance is provided under several schemes through its 41 regional/ branch offices spread over the country. Assistance provided directly for selling of new SSI units, Technology Up gradation and Modernizations, expansion, diversification, quality upgradation/acquiring of ISO 9000 series certification, Development of market for SSI products, Development of Infrastructure for SSI sector, Free shipment and Post shipment credit, and Export bill finance discounting of bills of manufacturing, Seller in SSI Sector. Selling either equipment or components and factoring services.

SIDBI offers financial assistance to different lines of Production, Modernization and Technological up gradation for these purposes TDMF (Technology Development and Modernization Fund Scheme) Scheme and Technology up gradation Fund Scheme in General and for Tanneries, Tannery Modernizations Scheme came to be lodged. For such SSI units engaged in manufacturing of selected products, capital subsidy on loans and advance to SSI units being provided by Scheduled Commercial banks SFCs and NSICL under credit linked capital subsidy scheme. Short term loans to electricity bonds to facilitate they purchases from SSIs and effect payments in time. Discounting of invoices of SSIs supplies. In addition to these schemes foreign currency assistance development and supporting servies enterprise promotion supporting measure etc came to be launched.

SIDBI in the year 1990-91 sanctioned Rs 2410 crores and disbursed Rs 1839 crores to SSI units. In the year 2004-05 the total sanctions of the SIDBI was Rs 9091 crores in total. During the same year total disbursement was Rs 6188 crores to SSI units of the country.The cumulative figures by 2004 –05 Rs 103496 crores was sanctioned and out of this Rs 69703 crores was disbursed. Likewise the Cumulative growth in Sanctioned amount and Cumulative growth in disbursements too has been given in the table below.

Table 3: SIDBI Share of SSIs in India (Cumulative Figures Amount Rs. In Crores)

Year	*Total Sanction Annual Growth %*		*Annual Growth Cumulative Sanction*		*Total Disbursements Cumulatve Disbursements*	
1990-91	2410	0	1839	0	2410	1839
1991-92	2847	18.13	2028	10.3	5257	3867
1992-93	2909	2.2	2146	5.8	8166	6013
1993-94	3356	15.4	2673	24.6	11522	8686
1994-95	4707	40.3	3390	26.8	16229	12076
1995-96	6066	28.9	4801	41.6	22295	16877
1996-97	6485	6.9	4585	-4.5	28780	21462
1997-98	7484	15.4	5241	14.3	36264	26703
1998-99	8880	18.7	6285	19.9	45144	32988
1999-00	10265	15.6	6964	10.8	55409	39952
2000-01	10821	5.42	6441	-8.12	66230	46393
2001-02	9025	-1.66	5919	-8.1	75255	52312
2002-03	10904	20.82	6789	14.7	86159	59101
2003-04	8246	-24.38	4414	-34.98	94405	63515
2004-05	9091	10.25	6188	40.19	103496	69703
CGR	103496	11.35	69703	9.37	657021	461487

Source: SIDBI Annual Report of 1990-91 to 2004-05 in India, Bangalore Branch, and Bangalore.

Graph 2 :

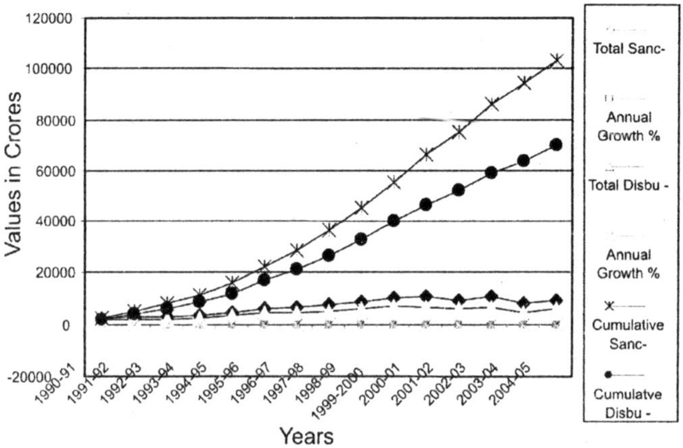

The annual growth rate, which stood at 1991-92 at 18.13. In the year from 1992-93 to 2004-05 the annual growth rate in sanctioned met with ups and downs even being with negative value annual growth stood at 10.25% by 2004-05.The Cumulative CGR by 2004-05 is being 11.35. In the disbursements also ups and downs appears very common. The cumulative percentage by 2004-05 stands at 40.19, but the cumulative CGR came down to 9.37. The cumulative figures of total sanctions & disbursements have been provided in the above table. The total Cumulative figures by 2004-05 were 657021 crores of rupees and the Cumulative disbursements were rupees 461487 crores in the same year. The figure points out a glaring difference with regard to Sanctions and Disbursements.

Our study is particularly with reference to the SSIs of Karnataka. As such we have to take into consideration the role of SIDBI with reference to SSIs of Karnataka in particular. In the year 1990-91 the total amount to overall SSIs Sector sanctioned amount was Rs 180.27 crores of rupees and disbursed Rs 138.26 crores of rupees. Specifically for SSIs out of this the sanctioned amount was 11941.65 lakhs of rupees in the year 2004-05. Out of which 96747.28 lakhs of rupees was sanctioned to SSIs in particular and disbursed Rs 82454.33 lakhs of rupees was sanctioned to SSIs in particular. Even in Karnataka it is clear that there is a gap between total sanctioned and disbursed. It becomes more glaring the percentages of total sanctions and disbursements. It is depicted in the table given here.

Table 4: Financial Assistance of SIDBI - Share of SSIs in Karnataka (Rs. in Crores)

Year	Total Sanctioned in India	Total Disbursements in India	Total Sanctioned in Karnataka	Percent	Total Disbursements in Karnataka	Percent
1991-92	2847	2028	210.51	7.39	167.4	8.25
1990-91	2410	1839	180.27	7.48	138.27	7.52
1992-93	2909	2146	217.57	7.48	199.71	9.31
1993-94	3356	2673	223.55	6.66	213.96	8.00
1994-95	4707	3390	296.57	6.30	224.2	6.61
1995-96	6066	4801	412.94	6.81	369.97	7.71
1996-97	6485	4585	457.18	7.05	274.48	5.99
1997-98	7484	5241	267.55	3.57	262.29	5.00
1998-99	8880	6285	1164.13	13.11	310.89	4.95
1999-2000	10265	6964	737.76	7.19	529.31	7.60
2000-01	10821	6441	1034.19	9.56	672.43	10.44
2001-02	9025	5919	824.18	9.13	791.84	13.38
2002-03	10904	6789	2140	19.63	1109.75	16.35
2003-04	8246	4414	1649.29	20.00	650.83	14.74
2004-05	9091	6188	969.4	10.66	826.35	13.35
Total	103496	69703	10785.09	10.42	6741.68	9.67

Source: SIDBI Annual Report of 1990-91 to 2004-05 in India, Bangalore Branch, Bangalore.

Graph 3: Financial Assistance of SIDBI - Share of SSIs in Karnataka (Rs. in Crores)

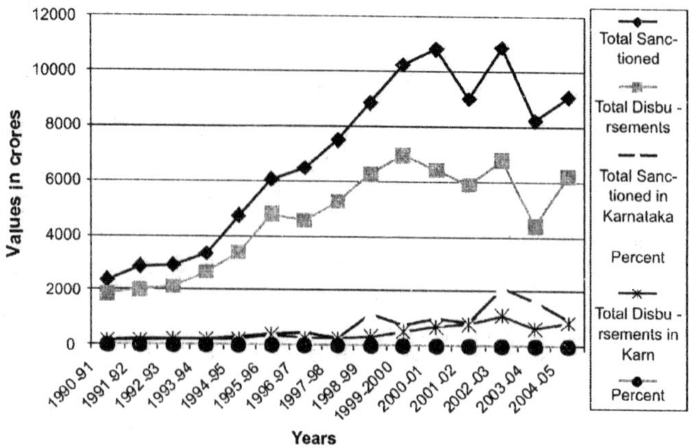

In Karnataka the total sanctions to SSI Sector in total went up to Rs 10785.09 crores . Out of which Rs 6741.68 crores . That is 62.51 percent out of total sanctions was disbursed. Specifically for the SSIs Rs 1010616.5 lakhs i.e., out of the total sanctions was ear marked for SSIs i.e 93.70 percent. Where as out of the total only Rs 618833.43 lakhs i.e, 61.23 percent was disbursed. The figures point out a glaring difference with regard to sanctions and disbursements

In Karnataka the total sanction to SSI sector in total went up to Rs 10, 78,576.52 lakhs out of which Rs. 6, 74,169.04 lakhs. That is 62.51 percent out of total sanctions was disbursed. Specifically for the SSIs Rs. 10, 10,616.5 lakhs i.e. out of the total sanctions was ear marked for SSIs i.e. 93.70 percent. Whereas out of the total only Rs. 6, 18,833.43 lakhs i.e. 61.23 percent was disbursed.)If we consider the region wise sanctioned and disbursements taking into consideration SIDBI as sanctioned and disbursed depending upon the geographical area of the state and the needs of SSIs of different states. The western region in the decade of 1990-91 to 2000-01 got a total sanction of Rs. 1 73,937.7 million was sanctioned and Rs. 1, 27,985.3 million was disbursed. This region was followed by Southern region, Northern region, Eastern region and Northeastern region.

Table 5: State and Region wise classification of loans disbursed SIDBI to SSIs during the period from 1990-91 to 2000-01 (Cumulative Amount Rs in Million)

State/Region	*Total Sanc*	*Percent*	*Total Disbu*	*Percent*
A-Eastern Region				
Bihar	6540.5	1.27	5797.8	1.51
Orissa	11174.9	2.17	8388.4	2.18
Sikkim	245.8	0.05	229.8	0.06
West Bangal	20333.6	3.94	14659.5	0
Andaman and Nicobar	4.2	0	5.1	0
Sub-total-A	38299	7.43	29080.6	7.56
B-North Eastern Region				
Arunachal Pradesh	116.2	0.02	109.1	0.03
Asam	1353.6	0.26	1127.5	1.29
Manipur	291.5	0.06	271.4	0.07
Meghalaya	437.7	0.08	357.5	0.09
Mizoram	106.6	0.02	105.9	0.03
Nagaland	137.8	0.03	134.9	0.04

Tripura	359.5	0.07	334.1	0.09
Sub-total-B	2802.9	0.54	2440.4	0.63
C-Northern Region				
Haryana	28792.3	5.58	20393.6	5.3
HIMACHAL Pradesh	3619.7	0.7	2932.7	0.76
Jammu & Kashmir	1582.6	0.31	1309.5	0.34
Punjab	19479.8	3.78	15500.7	4.03
Rajasthan	22369.2	4.34	15335.5	3.99
Uttara Pradesh	32638.7	6.33	25865.7	6.72
Chandigarh	2653.3	0.51	576.3	0.15
Delhi	29124	5.65	20725.5	5.39
Sub-total-C	140259.6	27.2	102639.5	26.68
D-Western Region				
Goa	6349.6	1.23	5094.1	1.32
Gujarat	65102.2	12.62	42843.3	11.14
MadhyPradesh	18148	3.52	14776.9	3.84
Maharastra	83170.7	16.13	64476	16.76
Dadara & Nagar Haveli	840.4	0.16	615.3	0.16
Daman & Diu	326.8	0.06	179.7	0.05
Sub-total	173937.7	33.73	127985.3	33.27
E- Southern Region				
Anda Pradesh	26080.2	5.06	19555.6	5.08
Karnataka	45505.5	8.82	35711.8	9.28
Kerala	25949.5	5.03	20718	5.39
Tamilnadu	62099.5	12.04	46054.1	11.97
Lakshadweep	1.1	0	0.9	0
Pondicherry	743.3	0.14	464.2	0.12
Sub-total-E	166379.1	31.1	122504.6	31.85
Total A+B+C+D+E	515678.3	100	384650.4	-

Source: SIDBI Annual Report of 2000-01 in India, Bangalore Branch, Bangalore.

Karnataka is in Southern region of SIDBI. In the decade pointed out Rs. 45,505.50 million was sanctioned and Rs. 35, 7111.80 million was disbursed to SSIs out of the total Rs. 1, 66,379.10 million sanctions. In Southern region the figure sanctioned in Karnataka governments to only 8.82 percent. Due to changes in the sanctioning policies of the region and the re-appropriations took place during the decade likewise out of the total sanction Rs. 35,711.80 million was disbursed. The disbursement out of the total amount disbursed in the region the disbursement of percentage in Karnataka stats at 9.28 percent. The totals of all the regions (i.e. five regions) the amount of money sanctioned to SSI sector by the SIDBI stands at Rs. 5,15,678.30 and disbursed Rs. 3,84,650.40 millions i.e. 9.28 percent.

Conclusion

The institutional network which has been created by Government of Karnataka and Central Government helped the SSIs of both backward and non-backward districts to get relief from the money lenders, who are notorious for charging accelerated rate of interest. No doubt the institutional network comprising IDBI/ SIDBI and other recognized financial institutions has been rendering immense help in catering to the credit needs of SSIs. In the course of the study it is noticed that the financial problems of SSIs, are not fully ameliorated. Especially financial constraints have posed a greater problem for proper flourishing of SSIs . As given in the tables of the chapter, it can be observed that there is unequal distribution of institutional finance for SSIs which have come up in different regions in India and Karnataka.. The SSI units which have come up in metropolitan areas/ urban agglomerations get major share in the financial assistance of public financial institutions. The beneficiary of SSIs even now face the problem of delay in loan sanction and disbursements, lack of transparency pertaining to sharing of information, inadequate loan powers given to the branch manager, collateral security problem; lack of propaganda about to credit schemes and others. On the lines of SIDBI, in Karnataka also there is need for modification of KSFC and other financial institutions to facilitate the SSIs to avail themselves of both working capital and long term capital through the single source also. There is necessity of starting SSIs, CBs to catering to the financial needs of SSIs.

References

P.R. Kulkarni, "Institutional Finance in the Development and Growth of SSI", Small Enterprises, Development and Management and Extension, Journal Volume 29, No.1, March, 2002, NISIET, Hyderabad, 30-41.

B. Yerram Raju, "Financing options: Banks and Small Industries", Financing India Vol XIX No.1, March 2005, New Delhi, 158-172.

Manoj Anand, (1993), "Economic Appraisal Industrial Projects, Schemes for Providing Financial Assistant", Deepa and Deepa Publications, New Delhi, 242-253.

Reserve Bank of India (RBI), (1969). "Report of the All India Rural Credit Review Committee". (Chairman: B.Venkatappa). Bombay: R.B.I.

Report on Trend and Progress of Banking in India Annual Reports from 1977 to 2004-05, Reserve Bank of India , Bombay.

Reserve Bank of India (RBI), "Credit Information Review" www.bankreport.rbi.org.in. R.B.I. Bombay

Reserve Bank of India (RBI), "FICCI study on, Bank Financing for the SSI Sector" www.bankreport.rbi.org.in. R.B.I. Bombay:

Bishnoi, T.R. (1991). "Policy Constraints and Banks Profitability: Impact of Priority Sector Credit". Indian journal of development banking. 9 (1 and 2). New Delhi.

Crook, clive (ed.) (1989), "Financial Systems and Development Industry and Finance" Series No.15, Washington: The World Bank.

Germidis, Dimitors and Others (1991). "Financial Systems and Developments: What Role for the Farmer and in formal Financial Sector". Paris: O.E.C.D.

Government of India, (G.O.I.), (1997). "Report of the Committee on NPA's of Public Sector Banks". (Chairman: A.T. Pannir Servan). IBA: New Delhi.

The Hindu, (2006), Karnataka Vikas Bank to Focus on SME Sectors", The Hindu, 5th June, 2006, Bangalore, p 4.

Mujumdar, N.A. (1996). "Financial Sector Reforms: An exercise in Arospection". Economic and Political Weekly, XXXI (II), Delhi.

Reserve Bank of India (RBI), (1978 to 2005). "Banking Statistics, Basic Statistical Returns various reports", Reserve Bank of India, Bombay.

A.G. Rohira, "Collapse of Credit Delivery Systems for Small Units", The Hindu Business Review, 10th December, 1997, Bangalore, p25.

CHAPTER 4

A Critical View of the Industrial Policy of Karnataka Since 1982-2011

Particular Reference to Small Scale Industries

A sustained economic growth of an economy is always guided by the principle of balanced economic growth. In a nutshell the balanced economic growth is nothing but an optimum growth of the major economic sectors of an economy. To realize this goal, the policy makers have to set appropriate goals of achievement in each and every sector of an economy. Having this view the Government of India too framed different policies since Independence. As a result the Indian economy has experienced profound changes and sustained growth in the last six decades. On the basis of the industrial policy announcement by the union government, the state governments have to frame their industrial policies. The Government of Karnataka too from time to time announced its industrial policy within the framework set by the central industrial policy to expand, direct and to monitor the industrial sector of the country. Let us glance at the different industrial policy announcement, particularly with reference to the SSIs in Karnataka.

The Industrial Policy of Karnataka1982-87

The government of Karnataka too framed its industrial policies to spread the industrial activities throughout the state since the dawn of independence. However to attract industries and to encourage investment in the nook and corners of the state. Particularly for SSIs, it framed and put to operation a comprehensive new package of incentives and concessions for investments in Karnataka, in the year 1982. This policy covered a period five years. This policy pronounced its objectives in clear-cut words the main objectives of this policy package may be put as- the dispersal of industries to backward areas providing inducements the industries of backward areas, it aimed at non-power, non-polluting and more labour -intensive industries. It also aimed at a target of establishing one lakh tiny, small scale and ancillary units by the end of sixth plan. Special incentives were given to SC/ST/Women and physically handicapped for the establishment of units. For the first time the policy aimed at the nine more taluks were included by the state where the eligibility of central subsidy was withdrawn for state subsidy of 15 percent subject to the maximum limit of capital investment of Rs 15 lakh. 62 Talukas in seven districts of Tumkur, Daskina Kannada, Uttar kannada, Gulberga, Hassan, Bijapur and Belagum came to be covered by a total subsidy of 25 percent. Out of this 10 percent being the central subsidy and 5 percent the state subsidy. Likewise the total subsidy provided to the industries of area covered under category A came to be 25 percent, for B 15 percent, for C 15 percent plus 10 percent for some 44 Talukas and 15 percent for other 28 Taluks. However this policy for the eligibility fixed Rs. 30 crores as limit of capital investment. The industrial policy took stock of different aspects of industrialization for the state extended a number of concessions. It is a policy which included specific guidelines to provide central and state subsidies to the tiny, small scale as well ancillary units. For investment subsidy it specified no capital subsidy limit for the industries coming in Zone-1. 10 percent subsidy for 44 Taluks subject to ceiling of rupees 5 lakhs and 15 percent subsidy for 49 Taluks subject to a ceiling of rupees 75 lakhs. For Zone-3, 15 percent subsidy for 41 Taluks subject to a ceiling of 7.5 lakhs. For industries in Zone-4 , 15 percent subsidy in 34 Taluks and 25 percent subsidy for 5 Taluks in Bidar district. In addition to the central subsidy a number of concessions were announced. Particularly with regard to development loan and working capital loan. Priority came to be given to certain category of Entrepreneurs. Seed capital assistance, term loans were recommended for on easy basis, repayment of loan on half yearly installments moratorium period of five years etc development of the local entrepreneurs.

The I.P. (Industrial Policy) of Karnataka particularly with reference to the SSI sector divided the state into different zones. The entire state was brought under four zones, such as zone –

I comprised of the areas where the industries are developed. The zone – II came to be regarded as the areas where the industries are less developed. The III – zone area is where the industrial growth has to be accelerated. The IV – zone, centrally declared industrially backward areas. The I. P. divided all the taluks under three categories as A, B and C. Category A covered 5 taluks of Bidar district came to be known as no industry districts. Category B compressed of 37 taluks of Mysore, Dharwar and Raichur came to be regarded as the taluks eligible for central subsidies. 68 taluks of Belgaum, Bijapur, Gulbarga, Hassan, Uttara Kannada, Dakshina Kannadaand Tumkur districts. This category came to be the remaining backward districts. On the basis of the categorization Government of India announced 25% investment subsidy for taluks in category A, 15% for the taluks coming under B, and 10% for the category C. The Central Government also announced other concessions including concessional finance for industries and some more concession for taluks industries in these backward areas. Later on 31-03-1983 for the industry of 9 taluks in backward districts were withdrawn to the industry where investment limits of Rs. 30 crores have exceeded. Later on some changes were made in this respect in the Govt. order 20. No. C12B SBC 83 Bangalore dated 31-10-1983. Subsequently the Government of Karnataka was specified. This policy provided reimbursement of registration fee Indian Standards Institution, commodity board etc subjected to maximum of Rs. 2000. In case of electricity tariffs 30% for the 1st year, 20% for the 2nd year, 10% for the 3rd year was declared as subsidy for the units on the actual energy charges paid by the units for all units consuming LT power for all units of different zones except unit of zone I. Subsidy was provided to a maximum of Rs. 25,000 for new SSIs ancillary units for the procurement of technical know how from different agencies excluding the units of zone I. This policy also provided subsidy for the purchase of generators to the extent of 10% in zone II, 15% in zone III and IV subject to a maximum of Rs. 5000 and Rs. 10,000 respectively. Price preference was given to all the tiny, small scale, and ancillary units to the extent of 15% for the first five year from the date of commencement of production. In addition to waving off the conversion fee, stamp duty exemptions, concessions in registration fee, subsidy for housing too were given. The Government of Karnataka also 50% sales tax concession for a period of 5 years for the products produced by industries of SSI sector. This policy intended to lay a strong foundation for the expansion of SSI units in most of the backward areas of the state. But the lack of knowledge on the part of the entrepreneurial class about the policy concessions. Majority of the entrepreneurs failed to make use of the subsidies and incentives provided by the industrial policy.

The Industrial Policy of 1990–95

On the basis of the earlier policy for the purpose of incentives and concessions, the state was divided into 4 zones. Zone I covering 2 taluks, zone II covering 38 taluks, zone III covering 129 taluks and zone IV covering 6 taluks and 3 growth centers to be setup during the period at Dharwar, Hassan and Raichur. Investment subsidy for new investment and for expansion, modernization and diversification of already existing units in zone II, III and IV was provided. 15% subsidy subject to maximum of 15 lakhs in zone II, 20% subject to maximum of 20 lakhs in zone III and 25% subsidy to a maximum of 5 lakhs in zone IV was provided to tiny, small medium and large scale industries on the basis of the value of their fixed assets. An additional investment subsidy of 25 lakhs to granted for all new industrial investments beyond 25 crores in fixed assets to be setup in zone III & IV. Sales tax concessions too made available for all units came to be established. Both CST and KST came to be exempted to the extent of 100% for units in zone II, for 3 years, in zone III for 4 years, in zone IV for 5 years from the date of commencement of commercial production for all tiny, small medium and large scale units in thrust sector. Later 100% exemption from the payment of entry tax for all the raw material components etc., was extended to export oriented industries. Special investment subsidy to the extent of 10% on the value of fixed asset subject to ceiling limit of 10 lakhs to the units proposed to be set in the EOIZ Bangalore and also to all 100 percent EOUS setup in zone II and zone III provided. However, the employment local labour to be the extent of at least 80% was set as a requirement exemption from payment of entry tax, exemption from power cuts by KEB and quality supply of power to these units to also provide. Additional concessions of 100%

EOUS to be set in EO 12 Bangalore and in zones II, III and IV from sales tax payable on all raw materials components, package materials consumables etc from the domestic tariff area was provided.

Additional import subsidy of 5% was provided to on capital investment for entrepreneur coming under SC/STs, minorities, women, physically handicapped and ex-servicemen. Units producing pollution control equipments and for utilization non con-ventional energy sources were provided an additional investment subsidy for 5% was provided subject to Rs.5 lakhs. Exemption on stamp duty and concessional registration charges waving of conversion fee, special incentive for revalidations of sick units were provided.

This policy, to a great extent though included many encouraging aspect, it suffered with some anomalies. Therefore the Government of Karnataka issued a new industrial policy in 1993. The defects experienced in the earlier policy came to be removed. Specific guiding lines were introduced in the new policy with regard to extending sales tax concessions, special concession for export-oriented units etc were introduced. Extending the currency of the policy up to 1998. However again the policy came to be revised, earlier in the 1996 itself. As such a new industrial policy was introduced in the year 1996.

The Industrial Policy of 1996-2001

The Government of Karnataka has announced a new policy 1996 and package of incentives and concession from period 1996-01 vide GO CIR/30/SPC/96 Bangalore dated 15-03-1996. This policy aimed at a greater acceleration in industrial development and to take the state to a prominent position in the industrial map of the country. The Government in the preamble of the policy itself said "the government has been pursuing a progressive Industrial policy and an attractive package of incentives and concessions. It indicated since 1991 there is a substantial investment flow into the industrial sector. This policy catalyzed and provided several new avenues for the free flow of investments with an objective to expand the industrial section to develop agro horticultural based industries to create employment opportunities for the available human resources, increase export of value added goods and services, encourage private sector for development of infrastructure, conserve the natural resources, affluent treatment and disposal to control pollution, encourage the utilization of non-conventional energy resources, develop skill among local youths, up-gradation of entrepreneurial training, improved productivity to encourage KIADB, KSSIDC, KEONICS, KSIIDC etc and along with voluntary organizations for infrastructure development. This policy announced several measures to provide marketing assistance to SSI units.

In order to achieve the various objectives and to provide grater incentives and concessions for tiny, SSI and ancillary industries including export of oriented units, the state has been divided into three zones. Such as-developed areas, which included Bangalore South and North Taluks and Bangalore urban agglomeration areas as per 1991 censes. This zone categorized as industrially developed. No incentives and concession in the form of investment subsidy was not provided. The II zone came to be called developing areas comprising 173 taluks excluding areas in zone I. This I.P. provided 25% investment subsidy subject to a ceiling limiting of Rs. 25 lakhs. The third zone called the growth centers which included Hassan, Raichur, Dharwad and other centers that is Mini Growth Centers proposed at Bijapur Ballary, Malur, Kolar District Nipani, Gadag, Chikamagalur, Chitradurga. Ancillary complex for steel plant project proposed at Thorannagual Ballery district. The units came to be established in this zone enjoyed an investment subsidy of 30% subject to a ceiling limit of Rs.30 lakhs. To encourage special categories of entrepreneurs that is SC/STs, minorities, women, physically handicapped and ex-serviceman. This policy also provided a special treatment for unit employing more than 50% of skilled professional women on a permanent basis for a period more than 3 years. To encourage investment for expansion diversification and modernization of existing units' special monitory benefits were made available. To develop industrial estates(Infrastructure), private cooperative organizations were offered an investment subsidy at the rate of 20% subject to Rs.20 lakhs for the promotion and establishment of Industrial estates. This subsidy was applicable for projects with a cost up to Rs.5 corers each, including the cost of industrial needs. Sales tax concession for new units, refund of sales tax for diesel used towards power generators, exemption for electricity cost, installation of equipments towards captive power generation too were made available. Exemption of CST and KST on sale of finished goods was made available to khadi and village industrial sectors. MEGA project which have an investments in fixed asset in excess of Rs.100 crores were provided for a special incentive package depending upon merit of each case special incentives for automobile manufacturing industry and special concessions for export oriented units to were made available in this policy. Exemption from stamp duty and concessional registration charges conversion charges too were given to tiny and SSI units, coming up in all areas other than in zone-I. This policy listed the units in different areas of production eligible for the incentive subsides and other concessions.

This policy looked into the SSIs sector in a wider prospective and had a generous soft corner for the development of SSI sector in the state.

The Industrial Policy of Karnataka 2001-2006:

The Government of Karnataka formulated a compressive Industrial policy in 1996 extending a package of incentives and concessions for new investors, by the end of 31st March 2000 the policy came to be modified. In all these years due to the encouragement provided to hi-tech industries in the key sectors like electronics, telecommunications. Information technology, procession engineering automobiles, ready made garments, bio technology and food processing registered a cognizable growth. Foreign investment came into the state in a considerable quantum between 1996-97 to 2001. The industrial sector witnessed a formidable change as shown in the table below.

Table 1: Achievements in the industrial sectors

Sl. No.	*Sector*	*No. of*	*Investment*	*Employment*
1	SSIs	93845	3008.78	444259
2	Medium Scale Industries	194	2499.96	45703
3	Large Mega Industries	21	8682.62	13331

Source: Department of Industries and Commerce Government of Karnataka.

This policy aimed at an achievement of economic growth rate at 9% for this an average growth rate of at 10 to 12 percent per year was proposed by the industrial policy. It had an objective of attracting Rs.20, 000 crore investments during the period of the policy and to have employment potential of at least Rs. 1.5 lakh per year. Several objectives were set and specific strategy was formulated to achieve the objectives. Like the earlier industrial policies, this policy too provided a large number of supportive measurers for the establishment and expansion of industrial units. Informative development on competitive basis was found a necessity the government established an infrastructure development fund with an initial capital of Rs.100 crores. Public/private partnership and private organizations were encouraged to develop Technology Park, Industrial estates, Industrial areas, Industrial corridor for focus sectors. Development of Industrial township for cluster industries was also given encouragement.

The KAIDB was entrusted with the promotion of five Agro Food Processing Parks. Two apparel Parks, a Special Economic Zone (SEZ), an Export Promotion Industrial Park, Three Auto Park, a Knowledge Park, dedicated to Biotechnology and related units and full pledged financial district near Bangalore. The government, for the first time provided the government land wherever available to KAIDB at free of cost to develop and provided allotments to entrepreneur at cheaper rates. KPTCL was encouraged to take steps to provide un-interpreted qualities power. This policy realizing the necessity of skilled and knowledge base workforce, different encouragements were provided to artisans training institutes, district training institute and polytechnic to upgrade the qualities and skill of men employed by SMEs its Strengthened SEDOK. Private organizations were encouraged to develop entrepreneurial training programmes. Specialized training institutes were established organizations like KUM came out as Nodal agencies to guide and provide assistance to entrepreneur to obtain the require clearances, consents, approval, registration/license etc from various departments. Fast track clearance, single window system came to help the entrepreneurs. The single window mechanism was stream lined to provide the needed assistance by units. This policy also provided various incentives and concessions. To administer this, the state was divided into 4 zones as developed area under A zone, developing area under B, backward areas under C and other zone D.

The details of investment subsidy made available to tiny and SSI units indifferent zone provided by the policy is pointed out in the table below.

Table 3: Investment Subsidy

Zone	*Particulars*	*Industry Sector Eligible for Subsidy*	*Investment Subsidy*
A	Developed Areas	Nil	Nil
B	Developing Areas	Tiny Industries	10% value of fixed assets subject to a Max. of Rs.5lakhs
C	Backward Areas	Tiny Industries	20% value of fixed assets subject to a Max. of Rs. 10 lakhs
D	As detailed in Annexure-1		Tiny and Small Scale Industries 25% value of fixed assets subject to a max of 12.50 lakhs

Source: Department of Industrie and Commerece Government of Karnataka.

In addition to this the policy provided the exemption from entry tax, concessional registration charges for land and shed, and a number of special concession too were provided. If you look at the provisions made by industrial policy of 2001-06 to peruse that the SSI units had a formidable encouragement in the state and a promising positive growth. But the state of affairs appears to totally different.

The Industrial Policy of Karnataka 2006-11:

The changed circumstances in the national economic front, the establishment and expression of certain segments of industrial sector and substantial inflow of capital forms abroad, necessitated a new look at the industrial sector in Karnataka. The government intended to achieve a growth rate in GSDP over 9% which called for an industrial growth of over 12% the state desired to increase its share in the National Export 15% to 20% by the end of this policy period. It aimed at the creation of additional employment to the extent of Rs.10 lakhs. With all these objectives the Government of Karnataka pronounced its new Industrial Policy of 2006-11. The new policy classified the state into three zones to administered incentives and concessions to tiny, SSI and ancillary unity.

Zone-1

79 taluks – most / more backward taluks as categorized by Dr. D.M.Nanjundappa committee Report.

Zone-2

85 taluks – [taluks not covered in zone 1 & 3]

Zone-3

12 taluks – Bangalore urban and rural districts [excluding taluks of Kanakapura and Magadi] Mangalore and Mysore taluks.

Government intended for the infrastructure development in 5000 acres per year during the policy period out which it intended 25% of the area for housing and other social infrastructure. The KIADB KSSIDC were strengthened and provided greater scope. This policy intended for the implementation of MEGA in water supply schemes. It encourage power generation by a comprehensive power policy.

This policy also to meet the raising energy requirement encourage gas distribution master plan, Special Economic Zone were encouraged in different urban district. Multi product SEZ in association with ONGC came to be established petroleum chemicals and petro-chemical investment region encouragement to industrial corridors, cluster development would be encouraged. Attention was focused for sub sector/areas where the state has core competency that is aeronautics space, engineering automobile, mechanical tool, steel, cement, pharmaceutical, food processing, apparel textiles, electronics information technology, bio-technology etc. This policy provided separate package for silk reeling industry. Renewable and non conventional sources of energy was another sector for development came to be recognized for the development of human resources incentives and concessions were made available for the establishment of training institutes. Food processing, agro food processing unit provided better treatment in the policy. Modernization and Upgradation was insisted upon in the context of globalization. Separate package was formulated for the revival of silk units. The BMRDA was provided encouragement to take up five new town ship around Bangalore. To implement self employment pro-grammes and self help groups DICs was designated as Nodal agency for the district. This policy for the purpose of global information to the benefit of entrepreneurs. Global information centre would be set up at all District Industry centers (DICs). Measures were contemplated in the policy for the imple-mentation of Kigarika Vikas scheme at an accelerated rate. Improved charkas would be provided to increase wage earnings by artisans. This policy also provided for government commit-ment to extend the facility of price preference of 15% for the purpose purchase and purchase preference made from SSI units. In order to achieve the expected export growth rate of 20% during the policy period VITC will be strengthened. The policy divided the state in to different zones to administer the subsidies/ incentives and concessions to tiny, SSI units.

The incentive of 25% value of fixed asset subject to a maximums Rs.15 lakshs per unit in the zone B and 20% of the value of fixed asset subject to a maximum Rs. 10 lakhs per unit in zone B. Additional subsidy of 5% of value of fixed asset subject to a ceiling of one lakh for special categories entrepreneurs would be given to all new units are to be set up during the policy period one aspects has to be taken into consideration in this policy is that this incentive is made available only to such units financed by KSFC/KSSIDC/Banks other financial institutions.

In addition to the above incentives a number of concessions were declared for the coming up industrial units exempting certain duties, tax fee etc. particularly this policy provided for exemption of electricity duty on captive power generation exemption of stamp duty on reduction of registration chargers, weaving of conversion charges, acquisition and allotment of land through KIADB subsidy for setting up of special treatment, plant, entry tax concession, liberal encouragement for human resource development, Infrastructure development facilities and techno-logical up gradation were declared.

The new industrial policy 2006-11 to look at, appears to be vary encouraging. The policy theoretically speaking is a well contemplated industrial policy, particularly from the point view of SSIs. It is a policy aimed at the overall development of the SSI units aiming at the realization of a balanced economic growth with reference to this section. Its goal to create large scale employment opportunities through human resource development programme appears to be price worthy. However the experience with regard to the implementation of the earlier policies provides ground to speak different. Even it may be, said that the earlier polices too went on in the same lines has the present policy but to a great extent they have failed at the hands of the bureaucrats who have to put the policy into operation in the true sense. Many many packages of subsides or incentives concessions might have been declared one has to accept, none of these, in majorities, have reached the hands of entrepreneurs. The entrepreneurs who are said to be more influential and those who have political affiliation and influence have grabbed the incentives and concessions. It has been come to the experience of investigators and researchers majority of the small scale entrepreneurial units and tiny units have not enjoyed the concessions. It is a real fact one. The experience had in Karnataka is note worthy to put here. At Mysore the Hebbal SSI association with the assistance of sate association organized an industrial adalath, then Deputy Chief Minister, (DCM) himself the finance minister was in the chair. Concerned officers were being present along with a large number of entrepreneurs of tiny and small scale units were present. One question came up before the adalath with regard to the issue of title deeds to tiny and small-scale units. Exempting the registration fees. The finance minister being himself the Deputy Chief Minister took decision to exempt the registration fee and specify one month or 30 days for the enjoyment of these concessions. Even though an officer at the secretariat level gave an adverse opinion the Minister exhibited his braveness and commitment to encourage the small entrepreneurs, himself being the finance ministers, he categorically directed all the officers to extend this facilities without taking into consideration the financial implications. He wanted the orders to be passed early in this regard. Though the bureaucrats does not give him a negative replay for him the intended order was passed very late and the KAIDB of Mysore district posed several hurdles and the DICs too co-operated with the KAIDB in negativeting the intension of the Deputy Chief Ministry, himself the finance minister of the state. This clearly indicates how the bureaucrats are able to negativeate and bring him all sorts of impediments in putting a desired policy into operation when the Minister himself was made to fail totally in his approach. How to expect a entre-preneur of a tiny and small scale units to get the incentives/subsidies or concessions from the burocratic grips.

In addition to this it becomes incomplete if we were not to say a word about the entrepreneurs. In majority of the cases entrepreneurs are unaware of the subside/incentives/concession provided by the state. Even it becomes highly impossible for entrepreneur of SSI, and tiny units to get sufficient information from the DICs and KAIDB officials. Such information generally kept secretes. Only be diverged at high state bribery. At every step, the small scale entrepreneur is put to a lot of exploitation at different levels. Even bricks and stones of the DICs and KIADB officers pose their demand. Then think of the officials. Therefore whatever the policy that the state promulgates it remains on the paper. To a great extent the entrepreneurs of tiny of SSI units are being frustrated. On paper in the name of industrial policy looks very encouraging, one who go through this comes with all appreciations but in reality it is a source of analyzing money for the bureaucrats of the departments concerned. This appears to be more glaring in the guidelines issued by the department to the concerned authorities.

REFERENCES

- Industrial Policy -1948-2005, Government of India.
- http.www.yahoo@co.in
- New Industrial policies of Karnataka, 1982-87, 1990-95, 1993-98,1996-2001,2001-06 and 2006-11.
- Report of SIDBI, (2004-05), Bangalore.
- Bhuleshkar A.V. and Mithani D.M (1993), "*Indian Economy in Transition Structural Reforms*" ANMOL Publications New Delhi.
- Development Commissioner (Small Scale Industries) Ministry of Small Scale Industries (2000) "SSI *in India the growth sector for the millennium*" published by the development commissioner (SSIs) Ministry of SSIs and Agro and Rural Industries Government of India.

- D'Souza C.M. (2001) *"Integratinag Environmental Management in SmallIindustries of India"* Electronic Green Journal, Issue 14, spring 2001 – Earthday.
- Jathar Y.B. and Beri S.G. (1939), *"Indian Economics"* Published Oxford University Press Humphrpy Mileford.
- Reserve Bank of India (1997), *"Report of the Expert committed on small enterprises"*, Supplement to RBI Bulletin Sept, 48&49.

CHAPTER 5

Present Industrial Policy of Karnataka, 2006-11 —A Critical Review

It is an accepted fact that a balanced economic growth is a topmost necessity for all the economies which have aimed at the high level growth rate and standard of living for their inhabitants. Indian economy with a large size of population, in any way cannot neglect the realization of a high growth rate. Agriculture and Industry happens to be the major sectors aided by other areas of development always are kept at alert to achieve a high level growth. Therefore, the government of India at the centre and states at the state level to achieve and maintain a continuous high growth rate suitable policies are to be formulated pertaining to different sectors of the economy. Realizing this, from time to time agricultural as well industrial policies have been framed and implemented.

In tune with the industrial policy of Government of India, Karnataka Government also, from time to time announces industrial policies in the state. In industrial sector the Government of India has framed a broad based industrial policy. Since 1948 the Government of India from time to time announced its policy statements till 1991. Later modified the same policy taking into consideration the changes that have occurred, till 2004-05. Therefore, it is clear the Government of India had a broad based industrial policy. This modified policy of 2004-05 is in operation. In order to remove the major problems such as poverty and unemployment of the country, it is to be remembered that the solutions are to be formulated to ensure a sustained economic growth on the basis of the principle of balanced economic growth. By building and strengthening the industrial sector of the country, the industrial policy is an essential guideline. The industrial policy of the Government of India serves as a broader guideline for all state governments to evolve their industrial policies. As such, the Government of

Karnataka too framed its industrial policies on the basis of the central industrial policy from time to time to assist, direct and monitor the industrial growth of the state. The government of Karnataka has pronoun-ced its industrial policy in the year 2006 covering a period of five years i.e. till 2011.

The Government of Karnataka in its new industrial policy intended to achieve a growth rate in GSDP over 9 percent which called for an industrial growth of over 12 percent.

The state desired to increase its share in the national exports from 15 percent to 20 percent by the end of the new industrial policy. It also aimed at the creation of employment opportunities to the extent of 10 lakhs. Totally speaking the present industrial policy of Karnataka aimed at putting down the problems — poverty and unemployment. This policy wanted to achieve a balanced sustained growth of the state's economy. With these objectives the industrial policy has been put in to execution from 2006. In nutshell, the present policy includes the different phases of industrial sector of the state, for its expansion and encourage-ment direction and monitoring. It includes all measures including assistance, subsidies, exemptions concessions etc to be given to the SSIs in particular and to all other industrial units, depending upon their size of investment, location, labour intensity, export capacity etc.

Categorisation of The Zones

The present industrial policy of Karnataka classified the state into three broad zones to administer and monitor its provision to tiny, SSI and ancillary units as—

Zone-I

79 taluks – most / more backward taluks as categorized by Dr. D.M.Nanjundappa committee Report.

Zone-2

85 taluks – [taluks not covered in zone 1 & 3]

Zone-3

12 taluks – Bangalore urban and rural districts [excluding taluks of Kanakapura and Magadi] Mangalore and Mysore taluks.

The details of the taluks shown under different Zones are given in the table below.

Table 1: Classification of Talukas in Karnataka into zones for the purpose of Administering Graded Scale of Incentives and Concessions

Sl. No	*District*	*Total No of Tqs*	*Zone-1 Most Backward Tqs.*	*More Backward Tqs.*	*Zone-2 Backward Tqs.*	*Zone-3 Industrially developed Tqs.*
1.	Bangalore(U)	4	-	-	-	Anekal
			-	-	-	Bangalore(North)
			-	-	-	Bangalore(South)
			-	-	-	Bangalore(East)
2.	Bangalore(R)	8	Kanakapur			
			Magadi	-	-	Channapatna,
			-	-	-	Devanahalli
			-	-	-	Doddaballapura
			-	-	-	Hoskote
			-	-	-	Nelamangala
			-	-	-	Ramanagram
3.	Chitradurga	6	Hosadurga	Hiriyur	Chitradurga	-
			Molakalmur	-	-	-
			Holakere	-	-	-
			Challakere	-	-	-
4.	Davanagere	6	Channagiri,	Honnali	Davanagere	-
			Harapanahalli	Jagalur	Harihara	-
5.	kolar	11	Bagepalli	Mulbagal	Kolar	-
			-	Gudibande	chikkaballapur	-
			-	Gwribidanur	siddalag	-
			-	-	hattamalur,	-
			-	-	bangarpet	-
			-	-	chintamani	-
			-	-	srinivasapura	-
6.	Shiomoga	7	-	Soraba	Shiomoga	-
			-	-	Bhadravathi	-
			-	-	Sagar,	-
			-	-	Shikaripur	-
			-	-	Hosanagar	-
			-	-	Thirthhalli	-
7.	Tumkur	10	Kunigal	Turuvekere	Tumkur,	-
			Madhugiri		Tiptur	-
			Gubbi, Sira	-	-	-
			Pavagada	-	-	-
8.	Chamarajanagar	4	Chamaraja	Gundlupet	Yelandur	-
			nagar	Kollegal	-	-
9.	Chickmagalur	7	-	Kadur	Chickmagalur	-
			-	-	Tarikere, Shringeri	-
			-	-	Mudigere, Koppa	
			-	-	Narishimarajapura	-
10.	Dakshina	-	-	Bantwal,	Mangalore	-
	kannada		-	Puttur	-	-

			-	Sulya	-	-
			-	Belthangadi	-	-
11.	Hassan	8	-	Arakagud	Hassan	
			-	-	Arasikere	-
			-	-	Channarayapatna	-
			-	-	Holenarishipur	-
			-	-	Belur, Alur	-
			-	-	Sakleshpura	-
12.	Kodagu	3	-	-	Madikeri,	-
			-	-	Somawarpet	-
			-	-	Virajpet	-
13.	Mandya	7	-	Malavalli	Mandya	-
			-	Nagamangala	Maddur	-
			-	K R Pet	Srirangapatna	-
			-	-	Pandavapura	-
14.	Mysore	7	H D Kote	Hunsur	Periapatna	Mysore
			-	T N Pura	K.R. Nagara	-
			-	Nanjanagud	-	-
15.	Udupi	3	-	-	Udupi,	-
			-	-	Kundapura	-
			-	-	Karkala	-
16.	Bellary	7	Sandur,	Siraguppa	Bellary	-
			Kudligi	H B Halli	Hospet	-
			-	H Hadagalli	-	-
17.	Bidar	5	Bhalki	Bidar	-	-
			Humnabad	-	-	-
			Basavakalyan	-	-	-
			Aurad	-	-	-
18.	Gulbarga	10	Sedam,	Gulbarga		
			Shorapur	-	-	-
			Yadgir	-	-	-
			Chitapur	-	-	-
			Afzalpur	-	-	-
			Shahapur	-	-	-
			Aland	-	-	-
			Chincholi	-	-	-
			Jewargi	-	-	-
19.	Koppal	4	Kustagi	Koppal	Gangavathi	
			Yelburga	-	-	-
20.	Raichur	5	Sindanur	Raichur	-	-
			Manvi	-	-	-
			Lingasugur	-	-	-
			Devadurga	-	-	-
21.	Bagalkote	6	Bilagi	Hunagund	Bagalkote	-
			-	Badami	Mudhol	-
			-	-	Jamkhandi	-
22.	Belgaum	10	-	Athani	Belgaum,	-
			-	Gokak	Khanapur	-
			-	Soundatti	Hukkeri,	-
			-		Ramdurg	-
			-		Bailahongal	-
			-		Chikkodi	-
			-		Raibag	-
23.	Bijapur	5	Muddebihal	-	Bijapur	-
			B bagewadi	-	-	-
			Indi, Sindgi	-	-	-
24.	Dharwad	5	-	Kalhghatagi	Dharwad	-

			-	-	Hubli	-
			-	-	Kundagol	-
			-	-	Navalgund	-
25.	Gadag	5	-	Mundargi	Gadag,	-
			-		Nargund	-
			-		Ron	-
			-		Shirahatti	-
26.	Haveri	7	-	Savanur	Haveri,	-
			-	Shiggaon	Renebennur,	-
			-	Hirekerur	Byadagi,	-
			-	-	Ha-nagal	-
27.	Uttara kannada	11	-	Supa	Karwar,	-
			-	Bhatkal	Haliyal,	-
			-	-	Sirsi,	-
			-	-	Mundagod	-
			-	-	Yellapura,	-
			-	-	Honnavar,	-
			-	-	Ankola,	-
			-	-	Siddapura,	-
			-	-	Kumta	-
	Total no of Talukas	176	39	40	85	12

Source: New Industrial Policy 2006-11, Department of Industries and Commerece Government of Karnataka , Bangalore)

Infrastructure Development

The State Government intended for the infrastructure development in 5000 acres per year during the policy period. Out of which it intended 25% of the area for housing and other social infrastructure. According to the new policy, the KIADB, KSSIDC are to be strengthened and provided greater scope. This policy intended for the implementation of MEGA projects in water supply schemes. It encourages power generation by a comprehensive power policy to meet the raising energy requirement. This policy also encourages gas distribution master plan; Special Economic Zones are also encouraged in different urban areas. For example, Multi Product SEZ in association with ONGC in the areas of petro-chemicals. The new policy calls for encourage-ment to industrial corridors, cluster development in different parts of the state. Attention is also focused for sub sectors/areas where the state has core competency i.e. Aeronautics, space engineering, automobile, mechanical tools, steel, cement, pharmaceutical, food processing, apparel textiles, electronics, information technology, bio-technology etc. This policy provided separate package for silk reeling industry. Renewable and non - conventional sources of energy is another sector for development came to be recognized, for the development of human resources incentives and con-cessions are made available for the establishment of training institutes. Food processing, agro food processing units are also provided better treatment in the policy. Modernization and up-gradation are insisted upon on the context of globalization. Separate package is formulated for the revival of silk units. The BMRDA is provided encouragement to take up five new town ships around Bangalore. To implement self employment pro-grammes and self help groups.

DICs are designated as nodal agency for the district. This policy, for the purpose of global information to the benefit of entrepreneurs, global information centre would be set up at all District Industrial centers (DICs). Measures are contemplated in the policy for the implementation of Kaigarika Vikas Scheme at an accelerated rate. Improved charakas would be provided to increase wage earnings by artisans. This policy also provided for government commitment to extend the facility of - price preference of 15% for the purpose of purchasing the products produced by SSI units. In order to achieve the expected export growth rate of 20% during the policy period VITC will be strengthened. As stated earlier, the policy was divided the state in to different zones to administer the subsidies/incentives and concessions to tiny and SSI units.

Capital Subsidy

The subsidy of 25% of the value of fixed asset subject to a maximum Rs.15 lakhs per unit in the zone B and 20% of the value of fixed asset subject to a maximum Rs. 10 lakhs per unit in zone B. Additional subsidy of 5% of value of fixed asset subject to a ceiling of one lakh for special categories entrepreneurs would be given to all new units are to be set up during the policy period. One aspect that is to be taken into consideration in this policy is that this incentive is made available only to such units which are financed by KSFC/KSSIDC/Banks other financial institutions.

Table 2: Other Exemptions and Concessions:

Sl.No.	*Type of Incentives*	*Small Scale Industries*
1.	Exemption of Electricity Duty on Captive power generation	Currently under Energy Department Policy Continued upto 2011.
2.	Exemption of Stamp Duty & Reduction of Registration charges	Zone-1: Full exemption. Zone-2: 75% exemptions. Zone-3: Nil. Stamp duty: In respect of loan & Credit deeds executed for availing term loans from FIs/ Banks & for execution of Lease, Lease cum Sale & absolute Sale Deeds by KIADB/ KSSIDC in respect of Industrial land/ plots allotted.Reduction of Registration charges: Concessional registration charges at Re.1 per Rs. 1000.
3.	Waiver of conversion fineL on lands converted for industrial use)	Zone-1: Full exemption subject to a maximum of 10 acres per unit. Zone-1: 75% exemptions subject to a maximum of 10 acres per unit. Zone-3: Nil
4.	Acquisition & allotment of land through KIADB	In respect of lands acquired for development of industrial area/ estates or single unit complex KIADB acquisition charges to be levied is 28% in respect of areas in Zone-3. For the areas in Zone-1& 2, acquisition charges would be 10%.
5.	Subsidy for setting up of Effluent Treatment Plants(ETPs)	One time capital subsidy up to 50% of the cost of ETP, subject to a ceiling of Rs. 100 lakhs per unit for all categories of industries for all Zones.
6.	Entry Tax & Special Entry tax concessions	Zone 1& 2; I) 'ET& Special ET exemption on "Plant & Machinery and Capital Goods" for an initial period of 3 years from the date of commencement of project implementation. For this purpose, the term "Plant & Machinery & Capital Goods" i.e., equipment etc which is put up in the power project units for captive generation of Electricity.

		II) On raw Zone-1& 2 e materials, inputs, component parts & consumables (excluding petroleum products) (where ever applcable0 for a period of 5 years from the date of commencement of commercial production. Zone-3:Nil
7.	Human Resource Developments	i) Grant up to 5 acres of Government land will be considered along with capital contribution of 50% of the project cost subject to a ceiling of Rs 2 crores per year for Training Establishment for sector specific training. ii) Recurring cost for running the training institution an amount of Rs 750/-p.m./ per trainee will be provided subject to a ceiling of Rs 15 lakhs per year for period of 3 years. iii) Government will launch a new scheme to provide Rs 750/-p.m.stipend with suitable matching contribution unemployed educated youth.
8.	Technology Upgradition	Zone1& 2:I) Existing scheme of 4% interest subsidy for TU loans availed from KSFC/ KSIIDC shall be extended to cover TU loans availed from Scheduled Commercial Banks, which are not covered under CLCS Scheme of Government of India. **Zone-1 ,2 & 3:** II) Existing incentives scheme for SSI units going in for BIS product certification or ISO series certification is continued with enhanced financial allocation. III) Encouragement to Patents Registration: Subsidy at 505 of the cost of tents registration, subject to a ceiling of Rs 2 lakhs per unit

Source: New Industrial Policy 2006-11, Department of Industries and Commerece, Government of Karnataka , Bangalore.

Critical Appraisal of Industrial Policy 2006-11

The new industrial policy 2006-11 to look at appears to be varying encouraging. The policy theoretically speaking is a well contemplated industrial policy, particularly from the point view of SSIs. It is a policy aimed at the overall development of the SSI units aiming at the realization of a balanced economic growth with reference to this sector. Its goal to create large scale employment opportunities through human resource development programme appears to be praise worthy. However, the experience with regard to the implementation of the earlier policies provides ground to speak different. Even it may be, said that the earlier polices too went on in the same lines as the present policy, but to a great extent they have failed at the hands of the Bureaucrats, who have to put the policy into operation in the true sense. Many packages of subsides, incentives and concessions might have been declared, one has to accept, none of these, in majority, has reached the hands of entrepreneurs. The entrepreneurs who are said to be more influential and those who have political affiliation and influence have grabbed the incentives and concessions. The subsidies and incentives declared by the government since long time remain undisbursed. Majority of the entrepreneurs of SSIs have expressed that the subsidies that are announced go into the hands of the bankers in the form of interest on loans that they have availed of from the banking institutions and KSFC. This has created an impression that the subsidies and incentives are being declared only to exploit the entrepreneurs pushing them into the obligations of bankers and KSFC. It is clear that no government funds have been allotted to clear of the subsidies and assistance declared in industrial policy to the entrepreneurs then and there only or at least during the period of the particular industrial policy. It appears the lack of commitment on the part of the concerned authorities. It has been come to the experience of investigators and researchers majority of the small-scale entrepreneurial units and tiny units have not enjoyed the concessions. It is a real fact, that one experience had in Karnataka is note worthy to put here. At Mysore the Hebbal SSI association with the assistance of state association organized an industrial adalath, and then the Deputy Chief Minister (DCM), himself the finance minister was in the chair. Concerned officers were being present along with a large number of entrepreneurs of tiny and small scale units. One question came up before the adalath with regard to the issue of title deeds to tiny and small-scale units, exempting the registration fees. The finance minister being himself the Deputy Chief Minister took decision to exempt the registration fee and specify one month or 30 days for the enjoyment of these concessions. Even though an officer at the secretariat level gave an adverse opinion the Minister exhibited his braveness and commitment to encourage the small entrepreneurs, himself being the finance ministers, he categorically directed all the officers to extend this facilities without taking into consideration the financial implications. He wanted the orders to be passed early in this regard. Though the Bureaucrats does not give him a negative reply for him, at that moment the intended order was passed very late and the KAIDB of Mysore district posed several hurdles and the DICs too co-operated with the KAIDB in negativating the intension of the Deputy Chief Minister, himself the finance minister of the state. This clearly indicates how the Bureaucrats are able to negativate and bring in all sorts of impediments in putting a desired policy into operation when the Minister himself was made to fail totally in his approach, how to expect a entrepreneur of a tiny and small scale units to get the incentives/subsidies or concessions from the Bureaucrats grips.

To attract and encourage the new entrepreneurs to the industrial sector. The new entrepreneur is to be given the required training. They have to be equipped with all the relevant knowledge and information required to be a successful entrepreneur. It is said it is possible by the Entrepreneur Development Programme. The programme that is going on in different centers has failed to realize the goal. This programme is being conducted in many cases on paper only. The agencies both government and private involved in importing the required knowledge only aimed at the grants that flow into their hands from the govern-ment. The people involved do not have the required knowledge and responsibility to bring up the new entrepreneurs. In these programs, mostly the people who are said to be trained are for the purpose of getting loans and other financial benefits under PMRY scheme. In this respect we have to say, people with commitment and sufficient suitable knowledge to be entrusted with training the new entrepreneurs.

In addition to this, it becomes incomplete if we were not to say a word about the entrepreneurs. In majority of the cases entrepreneurs are unaware of the subsidies /incentives/concession provided by the state. Even it becomes highly impossible for entrepreneur of SSI, and tiny units to get sufficient information from the DICs and KAIDB officials. Such information generally kept secret, only be divulged at high stake bribery. At every step, the small scale entrepreneur is put to a lot of exploitation at different levels. Even bricks and stones of the DICs and KIADB offices pose their demand, then think of the officials involved. Therefore whatever the policy that the state promulgates it remains on the paper. It is true, that at present to a great extent the entrepreneurs of tiny / SSI units are being frustrated. On paper in the name of industrial policy, the present industrial policy also looks very encouraging, one who go through this comes with all appreciations but in reality it is misnomer.

REFERENCES

1. Government of Karnataka (1982-87, 1990-95, 1993-98,1996-2001,2001-06 and 2006-11), New Industrial policy resolution of Karnataka, Bangalore: Directorate of Industry and Commerce
2. Government of India (1948-2005), Industrial Policy,. http.www.yahoo@co.in
3. Small Industries Development Bank of India (2004-05), Report of 2004-05, SIDBI, Bangalore.
4. Development Commissioner (Small Scale Industries) Ministry of Small Scale Industries (2000) "SSI *in India the growth sector for the millennium*" published by the development commissioner (SSIs) Ministry of SSIs and Agro and Rural Industries Government of India.
5. Jathar Y.B. and Beri S.G. (1939), "*Indian Economics*' Published Oxford University Press Humphrpy Mileford.
6. Reserve Bank of India (1997), "*Report of the Expert committed on small enterprises*", Supplement to RBI Bulletin Sept, 48&49.
7. Dr. Syed Vazith Hussain (2003), "*Small Scale Industries in the New Millennium*" published by prabhat Kumar Sharma for sarup and sons, Delhi P No. – 29.
8. Vasant Desai (1983), "*Problems and prospects of small-scale industries in India*", Himalaya publishing house – Bombay.

CHAPTER 6

Present Scenario of Small Scale Industries in Karnataka

Introduction

In Karnataka as industrialization gathered momentum so did increasing SSIs. SSIs play an important role in the economy of Karnataka, as they are labour intensive and create job opportunities for unemployed persons. They offer a higher productivity of capital than capital intensive industries, as they have low investment per worker. They help in spatial diversification in industrial development, rural development, and decentralization of economic power. Further, SSIs help to utilize locally available resources and provide suitable price for them. All this is required to increase and disperse economic growth. SSIs support entrepreneurial talent and skills, stimulate personnel savings, and help in developing innovative and appropriate indigenous technology, providing dynamism and contributing to competition. Hence SSIs have been given a very important role in the economic development of Karnataka and have been actively encouraged by offering a variety of institutional facilities, incentives and concessions. Thus an array of policy initiatives and procedural simplifications have been undertaken by the India and Karnataka Government to encourage the growth of SSIs, not only for creation of job opportunities but also to enhance their competitive capability. The governmental SSIs supportive measures include infrastructural support, provision for financial assistance for differential interest rates, duty concessions, technology upgradation, assistance to build entrepreneurial talent, facilities for quality improvement, supply of machinery on hire purchase basis, more and easier availability of needed raw materials, provisions for developed plots/industrial shed, marketing assistance, export intensive etc. Contributions of SSIs to Karnataka's industrial production, exports and employment are significant. About 321676 SSIs of Karnataka employing nearly 1828978 persons, account for about 35 percent of Karnataka's total exports and about 40 percent of industrial manufacture (2005).

Changing Concept of SSIs in India and Abroad

The SSI Sector owes its definition to the INDUSTRIES [Development and Regulation) ACT 1951. This sector is defined in terms of investment limits in plant and machinery in their original value, up to a prescribed value. The SSIs sector comprises a widely divergent spectrum of industries, ranging from the micro and rural enterprises using rudimentary technology on one hand to the modern SSIs using sophisticated technology on the other.

The definition of SSIs usually depends upon the socio-economic conditions of the country and the programme adopted. Some governments stress to develop artistic crafts and skill while in others crafts are excluded. The industries which are considered as small in highly developed countries might be considered as medium or even large in a developing country. In USA, the number of workers alone is the criterion in defining the small business, whereas, in Japan both capital limit and the number of workers are considered. India has adopted capital as the basis for defining the small industries. The USA or Japan have not changed their criterion because of their economic stability and industrial maturity, while India has changed the scope once and the capital limits four times because of the rapid changing requirements of the SSI sector. In 1952, the Committee of Economic Commission for Asia and Far East [ECAFE] had suggested that for statistical purposes, the establishment employing 20 workers when using electric power or 50 workers when they are not using electric power, be defined as SSI. The 'cottage' and 'small scale industries' were considered 'indigenous' or 'native' and were used in the common parlance in composition with large scale industries established in India under western influence. The village and small scale industries cover a wide range, which differ in the nature of their products, scale and technique of production, location and channels of distribution. More details of SSIs in other countries are given in Table - 1.

Table I: Definition of Some in Asia and Other Countries

Country	*Category of Industry*	*Criteria*
China	SME	Depends on product group; investment ceiling 30 million Yuan (US$8million)
Germany	SME	No size definition. Crafts firms are members of craft Chambers and are defined by types of businesses and the qualifications of master craftsman. About 95 percent of small firms have an employment of less than 20 workers.
Japan	Manufacturing	Less than 300 employees and capitalization less than 100 million Yen
	Wholesale Trade	Less than 100 employees and capitalization less than 30 million Yen
	Retail Trade and Services	Less than 50 employees and capitalization less than 10 million Yen
Mexico	Micro	Less than 15 employees and gross Income /Sales less than US$175000
	Small	15-99 employees and gross income / Sales less than $175000
	Medium	100-249 employees and gross income / Sales less than $3500000
Malaysia	SMIs	Employment less than 75 full time workers or with a share holder fund of less than RM 2.5 million (US$1.0 million)
	SIs	Manufacturing establishments employing between 5 and 50 employees or with a share holders fund up to RM 500000
	MIs	Manufacturing establishments employing between 50 and 75 full time employees or with a share holders fund between RM500000 to RM 2.5 million
Taiwan	SMEs	In manufacturing, paid up capital less than NT$60 million or number of regular employees not to exceed 200.

	SSEs	In manufacturing, regular employees not to increase 20
South Korea	Small	Less than 20 employees
	Medium	20-300 employees. In some categories up to 700 employees. With assets of up to US$700000(80bn Won)

Source: *SIDBI, (1999), Report on Small Scale Industries Sector, Small Industries Development Bank of India, Lucknow, P.26. * *Handbook on Foreign Direct Investment by small and medium sized enterprises- Lesson from Asia, UNCTAD, Geneva.1998

At present, in advanced industrialized countries as well as in emerging developing economies SMEs are recognized as a key source of dynamism, innovation and flexibility. It is a worldwide accepted phenomena that SMEs are responsible for most net job creation in OECD countries and contributing important contributions to innovation in productivity and economic growth. Even in case of defining SMEs different quantitative criterions are taken into consideration. As a result the definitions adopted by different countries differ from one another as shown above.

The entire industrial activity in India has been divided into factory and non-factory sector. The industrial units with 10 or more workers using electric power and 20 or more workers not using power are all factories. The factories are registered under the Indian Factories Act, 1948. The village and small scale industries have been categorized in six broad groups namely handloom, sericulture and silk, coir, handicrafts, khadi and village industries and small scale industries although these categories sometime overlap. The first attempt to study the problems and prospects of village and small scale industries at the national level was made by the National Planning Committee [NPC] in 1938. Soon after the National Government was formed, as a measure of first step, a conference of SSIs was held in December 1947, which discussed in detail the problems and the revival of cottage industries. Realizing that it was a difficult task for a single agency to co-ordinate with large and varied groups of industries, the Government of India set up such All-India Boards as the All India Handloom Board [October, 1952], the All India Handcrafts Board [November, 1952], the Coir Board [July, 1953], All India Khadi and Village Industries Board [February,

1953], and the Small Scale Industries Board [November, 1954], to coordinate all activities regarding SSIs. The Boards so constituted were made responsible to coordinate and develop village and small scale industries. In 1977, there was a demarcation of a sub-sector in the SSIs sector, known as 'tiny industries', initially defined as those with corresponding investment of not more than Rs one lakh and situated in places with a population of less than 50,000. Subsequently, the capital limit in respect of tiny industries has been raised to rupees two lakhs with no change in population limit. In short, these are now three sub sectors, tiny industries, SSIs and ancillary industries.

Thus during the years 1955-80, the definition of SSIs has been revised as many as five times due to the changing requirements of the SSI sector. During these 25 years, the investment limit has been raised from Rs 5 lakhs to Rs 20 lakhs to achieve the broad based policy objectives. There had been some criticism on the Government's definition in August 1980 that the States were not consulted and the implications were not properly analysed. The Government considering the significant price rise that occurred during the preceeding five years while raising the investment limits.The concepts of ancillary and tiny units were introduced in 1960 and 1977 respectively. Small Scale Service Establishment [SSSEs] were first classified in 1985 and later redefined, in 1991 as Small Scale Services and Business Enterprises [SSSBEs]. The definition of women entrepreneur's enterprise was brought out in 1988 and modified in 1991. The periodic revision in the definition of SSI, as defined by the Government of India are presented in the Table 2.

Definition of SSIs In India

Table 2: Definition of SSIs In India

Year	*Investment limits*	*Additional conditions*
1950	Up to Rs. 5.00 Lakh in fixed assets	Less than 50/100 persons with or without power
1960	Up to Rs. 5.00 Lakh in fixed assets	No condition
1966	Up to Rs. 7.50 Lakh in Plant and machinery	No condition
1975	Up to Rs. 10 Lakh in plant and machinery	No condition

1980	Up to Rs. 20 Lakh in plant and machinery	No condition
1985	Up to Rs. 35 Lakh in plant and machinery	No condition
1991	Up to Rs. 60 Lakh in plant and machinery	*SSSBEs upto Rs. 5 lakhs. The location specific condition was withdrawn. The **SSSEs classification was suspended in 1991 and replaced by the term SSSBEs.
1997	Up to Rs.3.00 crore in plant and machinery	No condition
1999	Up to Rs.1.00 crore in plant and machinery	No condition
2005	Up to Rs.1.00 crore in plant and machinery	No condition

SSSE* – Small-Scale Service Establishment **SSSBE – Small-Scale Service and Business (Industry Related) Entrepreneurs. * Government of India (2000&2005), *"SSI in India the Growth Sector for the Millennium,* Present Definitions (w.e.f.24.12.1999) Development Commissioner, SSIs Annual Reports of SIDO for 1992-93 to 2003-04.((New Delhi: Small Industries Development Organization, Ministry of SSI's, Government of India).

This indicates, in India as time and circumstances demand the definition of SSI underwent modifications. Look at the literature on SSIs in India, the definition and composition of the sector is based on investment ceiling on the original value of installed plant and machinery. The Government of India has adopted official definition of modern SSIs, which happens to be the latest with reference to all the five categories of SSIs, namely.

1. Small Scale Industries SSIs
2. Ancillary Units
3. Tiny Units
4. The Small Service and Business (Industry Related Enterprise (SSSBE).
5. Women Enterprises
    1. SSIs in India are defined in terms of units for which investment on fixed asset such as plant and machinery, whether on ownership basis or lease or hire purchase, does not exceed Rs. one Crore.

2. Ancillary industry is that industrial undertaking which is engaged in the manufacturing of parts, components, sub – assemblies, tools or intermediaries or the rendering of services and the undertaking supplies or proposes to supply not more than 50 percent of its production or services, as the case may be, to one or more other industrial undertakings and whose investment in fixed assets in plant and machinery, whether held on ownership terms or on lease or on hire purchase, does not exceed Rs. one crore.
3. Tiny units are those units having investment in plant and machinery not exceeding Rs. 25 Lakh irrespective of location.
4. The SSBE is said to be industry related to service and business enterprises having investment in plant and machinery excluding land and building up to Rs. 51 Lakh irrespective of location.
5. Small Scale Unit where one or more women entrepreneurs have not less than 51% financial holding, on the condition that a Small Industry cannot be owned, controlled or be a subsidiary of another industrial undertaking.

SSIs in Karnataka during the Pre-Independence Period-a brief analysis

Before the advent of the industrial revolution, the type of SSIs which existed in Karnataka were mostly handicrafts and limited to cottages. It had been observed in 1804 that there existed 1,30,942 looms including 34,800 Kambali loom, 9134 salt manufactures, 52 brass workers, 853 iron forges and 2991 oil mills in the erstwhile Mysore State. In other areas too these crafts flourished.During the nineteenth century these industrial enterprises lingered on, despite the industrial revolution though without much encouragement or patronages by the state. In 1881, the state government took active interest in nursing the indigenous skills for creating wealth.

The establishment of the first Government Industrial School at Mysore in 1882 and another at Hassan in 1889 to impart manufacturing knowledge and to foster certain traditional skills such as carpentry, smithy, rattan work, etc., which even to-day find pride of place in Karnataka, bears eloquent testimony to the concern of the government for promoting manufacturing activities. In the subsequent years, the state government established Artisan Training Institutes in all the districts of the state to foster the traditional crafts and skills. After the economic conference in 1911, the government followed a policy of increasing the number of skilled workers and multiplying their occupations. Manufacture and trade, the chief instruments for increasing wealth, were specially encouraged, skilled workers were trained in wood, iron, clay, leather and textiles and all endeavour was made to provide the people with their every day cardinal wants. In pursuance of a policy, the government went to the extent of even sponsoring industrial exhibitions to encourage manufacture.

In 1912, with Sir M. Visveswaraya as Dewan of Mysore, a new area of industrial activities began. The newly founded Department of Industries and Commerce set out to encourage certain artisan-oriented manufacturing activities. To increase the productivity in SSIs people were helped to introduce simple but improved tools and machines. Later Dewan, Kantaraja Urs showed keen interest in village industries. The freedom movement and the spirit of swadeshi and self- reliance fostered by it, gave a fillip to small- scale and village industries. Dewans like Sir Mirza Ismail had been influenced by the thoughts of Mahatma Gandhi in this regard. The Congress Ministries that came to power in 1937 in British Presidencies, and after 1947 in the whole country paid special attention to SSIs and decentralization . The five-year plans and programmes to give a boost to this sector.

Products Manufactred by SSIs of Karnataka State

The SSIs sector has grown steadily over the years, and presently occupies a very important place in the economy of Karnataka state. The contribution of the SSI sector in terms of generation of employment, output and export is quite significant. The number of registered SSIs in the state has increased from 19908 in 1980 to 321676 in 2005. These numbers are exclusive of units in the unregistered sector. The total investment of this sector was Rs

18666.18 lakhs in 1980. It increased to Rs. 691969.68 lakhs in 2005. Infact all these years, the SSI sector has achieved a rate of growth higher than that of overall industrial sector. With regard to employment, the number of persons directly employed by SSIs sector has increased from 266956 as in 1977 to 1828978 persons at the end of march 2005 .The SSI sector in Karnataka has shown good performance in the field of export sector also. Exports stood at Rs. 55886.02 crores at the end of March 2006.

The variety and range of products produced by the Karnataka's SSI sector reflect the amazing progress made in this decentralized sector. From the ordinary products that they were producing during 1940s, and 1950s, engaged either in the production of traditional articles or undertaking repair works and service facilities, presently SSIs have stunningly emerged as versatile and modern units. In other words the SSIs of Karnataka manufacture the items right from small pins to big plane parts, subassemblies, tools, Zigs etc

In Karnataka SSI units have been categorized by Government of Karnataka into 17 broad groups by the Directorate of Industry and Commerce. The details of this categorization of board groups, the number of SSIs and percentages of different categories of SSIs in the state as on 31st march 2005 are presented in Table .3.

Table 3: Classification of Registering SSIs of Karnataka (Cumulative) As on March, 2005.

Sl. No.	*Classification of Industries (Major Head)*	*No. of Units*	*Percentage (%)*
1.	Food & Beverages	41886	13.02
2.	Textiles & Garments	45250	14.07
3.	Wood & wood products	43572	13.55
4.	Printing & Stationery	11100	3.45
5.	Leather & Leather goods	12538	3.90
6.	Rubber & Plastics	7404	2.30
7.	Chemicals	9727	3.02
8.	Glass & Ceramics	7016	2.18
9.	Basic metal & Metal products	12575	3.91
10.	General Engineering	23696	7.37
11.	Electrical & Electronics	9703	3.02

12.	Automobiles	2312	0.72
13.	Transport & Equipments	1228	0.38
14.	Ferrous & Nonferrous	s1396	0.43
15.	Job work & Repairs	26911	8.37
16.	Other Services	20637	6.42
17.	Miscellaneous	44725	13.90
	Total	321676	100.00

Source: Directorate of Industries and Commerce, Government of Karnataka, Bangalore.

As shown in Table-3 the total number of registered SSIs stood at 321676 at the end of 31st march 2005. Out of the total number of SSIs in the state, textiles stands first in the state [14.07%]. The next largest number is miscellaneous units which constitute 13.90 percent. Wood and wood products numbering 43572 constitute 13.55% of the SSI units of the state. Food and beverages units occupy the 4th place. Job works and repairs occupies 5th place [8.37%]. General engineering occupies 6th place. Next come the other services units. The percentage of leather and leather goods, printing and stationery, rubbers & plastics, chemicals, glass & ceramics, metal & metal products, electrical & electronics/the range between 3.02 percent and 3.90%. Automobiles transport & equipments, ferrous & non-ferrous units range between 0.38% and 0.72%.The category of food and food products include those undertakings which are engaged in food items, pickles, pappads, fruit juices, lime and lime products, dairy products, ice cream, dal making, wheat flour etc.The SSIs belonging to the category of textiles and garments manufacture products such as industrial fabrics, silk thread, silk reeling/ twisting, and manufacturing of twisted fabrics, production of handloom, silk and cotton sarees, synthetic cloth including dupian cloth. Power units engaged in the production of silk sarees also come under this category. Under wood & wood products category a variety of wood & wood products are produced. Majority of entrepreneurs are following this for generations who have learnt the skill from their parents. Furniture items, electrical meter boxes, beading items, RCC roof-lintel items are included in this category. The category of printing & stationery is an industry of small firms using simple technique of letterpress to the one with imported offset printing. Present increased commercial activities, growing use of printed wrappers, paper bags, etc. The category of leather & leather goods include those undertakings which are engaged in leather items, footwear etc.The category of rubber products such as moulded goods, extruded rubber parts and components and foam products are made by small scale units. The category of Plastics are not only substituting other conventional materials in automobiles, radios, telephones, transportation sector etc., but they are also used in machines as components. They have substituted so many metals like steel, copper, bronze and also wood, rubber, leather etc. The category of Glass and Ceramics include those undertakings which are engaged in granite, mosaic & bricks, tiles statues. General engineering category includes, machine tool accessories, pressing components, precision turned components, taps, hand tools, watch cases, gear boxes, fabrications of doors, shutters, grills and other industrial equipments like cranes, mixers etc are included in this group. Sheet metal fabrication, industrial components, automobile parts, submersible pumps and valve operators are also come under this category. The category of electrical & electronics, a wide variety of electrical equipments and machinery such as motors, switchgears, wiring accessories, transformers, cables, domestic electrical appliances, street light fittings, voltage stabilizers, Aluminum and Copper, conductors etc., are now being manufactured successfully in the small scale sector. Automobiles industries include pressed multistory steel fabricated items, Tabular seat frames and legs. Ferrous and Non-ferrous category include, Aluminum utensils, Name plates, Alloy castings, metal profile products etc. Under Jobworks & repairs/services category variety of job services and repairs are done. From simple to complicated work there are different varieties of job work are undertaken, which provide self-employment opportunities as well as employment to others depending upon the type of work. Motor rewinding, automobile servicing and repairing of automobiles and machines are undertaken under this group. The category of other services includes those undertakings which are engaged in maintenance. repair, testing or servicing of all types of vehicles and machinery of any description including electronic/electrical instruments i.e., measuring/control instruments, televisions, tape recorders etc.

Growth Patterns of SSIs in Karnataka (Registered Units)

The significance of SSI sector in the economic scenario of the state is well exhibited in the analysis of its growth and spread in the state. The sectors role in creating employment opportunities and avenues for investment are also very significant. A Comparative study of these dimensions of the SSI sector of Karnataka before and after the ERs has been made clear in the following pages.

Pre-reform Period							Post-reform Period						
Year	No of Units	Rate of Growth	Capital Investment (Rs in Lakhs)	Rate of Growth	Persons Employed	Rate of Growth	Year	No of Units	Rate of Growth	Capital Investment (Rs in Lakhs)	Rate of Growth	Persons Employed	Rate of Growth
1977-78	1621		1517.11		24822		1991-92	10588		18623.11		61903	
1978-79	2075	28.01	1450.74	-4.37	16957	-31.69	1992-93	11368	7.37	19772.5	6.17	62835	1.51
1979-80	2910	40.24	3255.01	124.37	24376	43.75	1993-94	12614	10.96	19890.56	0.60	69563	10.71
1980-81	2776	-4.60	3042.37	-6.53	21357	-12.39	1994-95	13503	7.05	26463.26	33.04	73999	6.38
1981-82	3396	22.33	4954.7	62.86	29214	36.79	1995-96	11856	-12.20	33160.01	25.31	70903	-4.18
1982-83	6096	79.51	2793.82	-43.61	31420	7.55	1996-97	13529	14.11	35811.37	8.00	67631	-4.61
1983-84	7479	22.69	6397.01	128.97	36314	15.58	1997-98	34402	154.28	66450.96	85.56	132978	96.62
1984-85	8073	7.94	6324.31	-1.14	55849	53.79	1998-99	13422	-60.98	59752.12	-10.08	69579	-47.68
1985-86	11634	44.11	8787.09	38.94	60796	8.86	1999-2000	15938	18.75	73705.58	23.35	88279	26.88
1986-87	11179	-3.91	9408.51	7.07	56888	-6.43	2000-01	16554	3.86	65157.83	-11.60	85792	-2.82
1987-88	10530	-5.81	10165.09	8.04	52498	-7.72	2001-02	16964	2.48	47883.6	-26.51	73195	-14.68
1988-89	9811	-6.83	10532.77	3.62	50448	-3.90	2002-03	12029	-29.09	40836	-14.72	57371	-21.62
1989-90	9700	-1.13	11247.02	6.78	51521	2.13	2003-04	12220	1.59	37054	-9.26	56790	-1.01
1990-91	9884	1.90	11843.16	5.30	53568	3.97	2004-05	11238	-8.04	38541	4.01	49998	-11.96
Total	**97164**	224.44	**91718.71**	**330.29**	**566028**	**110.30**		**206225**	**110.14**	**583101.9**	**113.87**	**1020816**	33.52
A.A.G		**1603.14**		**2359.2**		**787.86**			**786.71**		**813.36**		**239.43**

Graph 1: Before ERs: Registered SSIs in Karnataka, Their Capital Investmenst and Number of Persons Employed

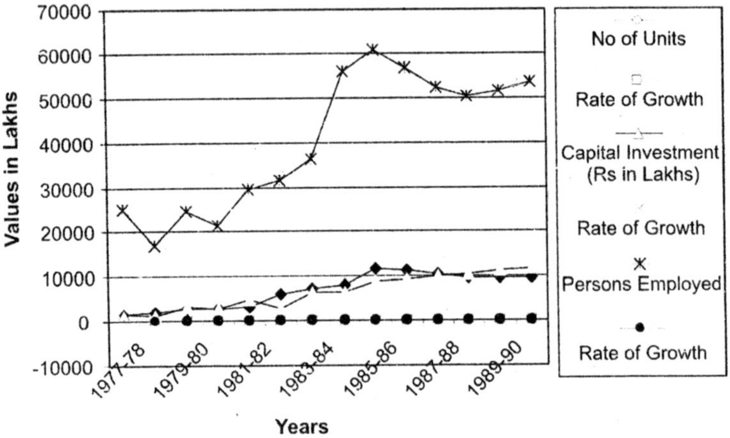

Graph 2: After ERs: Registered SSIs in Karnataka, Their Capital Investment and Number of Persons Employed

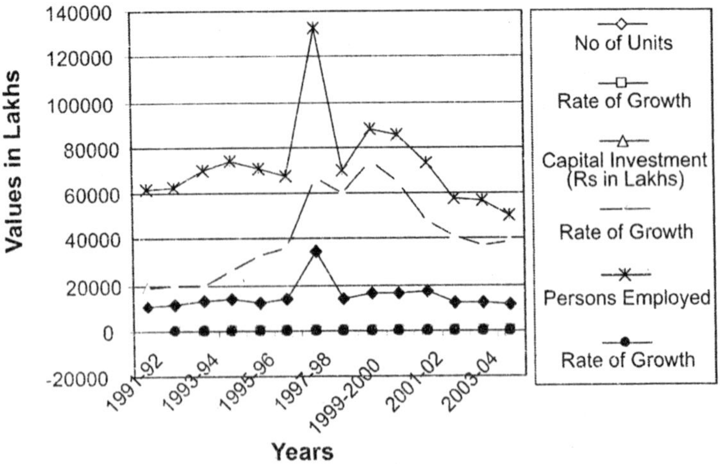

The total number of units registered in the state in the year 1977-78 stands at 1621. In the year 1985-86the number of units registered appears to be the highest i.e., 11634 fallowed by 11179 units in the year 1986-87 and a bit less i.e., 10530 units in the year 1987-88. In all the years from 1977-78 to 1990-91 the number of units registered remained only in the four digit figures. The rate of growth in the year 1982-83 stands at 79.51 fallowed by 44.11 percent in the year 1985-86, followed by 28.1 in the year 1978-79 and 22.69 percent in the year 1983-84 and 22.33 percent in the year 1981-82, in all the other years the growth rate remained negative except in the year 1984-85 and 1990-91 being 7.94 percent and 9.10 percent respectively. Whereas the states average growth rate between 1977-78 to1990-91 stands at 1603.14 .In the capital profile the total amount of capital invested in the state in this sector is 1517.11 lakhs of rupees and the figure in the year 1990-91 shot up to Rs 11843.16 lakhs. The total amount of capital invested in the sector at the end of the period stands at Rs 91718.71 lakhs. The investment growth rate is highest in the year 1983-84 i.e., Rs 128.97 lakhs of rupees. In the year 1979-80 it is Rs 124.37 lakhs. Fallowed by 62.86 lakhs in the year 1981-82and Rs 38.94 lakhs in the year 1985-86. Leaving 1978-79, 1980-81, 1982-83 and 1984-85 varying the growth rate in the investment being negative i.e., (-) in all other years. The volume of employment in the SSI sector in the year 1977-78 the number of persons employed were 24822. In the year 1990-91 the number of persons employed was 53568. Taking into consideration the total employed at the end of 1990-91 stood at 566028 persons. During the period 19977-78 to 1990-91 the average increase in the employment growth rate was 787.86. However except for few years the sector instead of creating employment it has dispensed with employees.

The statistics available for the post ERs period exhibits a picture different from the pre ERs period. Number of units after the ERs put to operation. I.e., in the year 1991-92 stood at 10588. We have to note down here one aspect i.e., they were already 9884 units were inexistence in the year 1990-91 i.e., before the ERs came into operation. Except for year 1997-98 the number of units registered were 34402 fallowed by 2001-02 and 2000-01 the number of units registered stood at 16964 and 16554 respectively. The growth rate stood at 154.28 in the year 1997-98. Except for the year 1999-00, 1996-97, 1993-94 where in the growth rate though positive it is not cognizable. Whereas for all other years after the ERs came into force up to 2004-05 the growth rate indicates negativity i.e.,(-). Even with regard to the total growth rate before the ERs came into force it was 224.44. But after ERs came into operation it came down 110.14 in the period of study. It is more glaring if we look into the average growth rate (AGR) figures. The AGR was 1603.14 before the period of ERs. Where as after the ERs (for the study period) it's stood at 786.71 i.e., more than 50 percent units declined in growth rate in the post reforms period.

With regard to the total capital invested, before the ERs came into operation the total capital invested in the year 1990-91 stands at Rs 91718.17 lakhs, the growth rate being Rs 330.29 lakhs whereas the average growth in the capital invested between 1991-92 to 2004-05 stood at 813.36. This indicates there is a formidable fall in the growth rate of investment as well the average. Even though there is a rise in the total capital invested. Where as after ERs came into operation in the year 2004-05 the total capital invested in the sector is Rs 583101.9 lakhs the growth rate was only Rs 103.87 lakhs. In the employment also the trend is a sharp decline. In the year total persons employed in the sector before ERs came in to force were 506628. The growth rate being 110.30 and the average growth rate in the employment in SSI was 787.86. Whereas after the ERs came into operation by 2004-05 the number of persons employed stood at went up to 1020816 but the state average came down from 787.86 in the year 1990-91 to 239.43 by 2004-05.

All these figures indicates a declining trend in the SSI sector with regard to number of units capital invested and the number of employed in the sector. Even though there is sum increase not cognizable after the ERs came into operation.

Problems of SSIs in Karnataka

Even though the development of SSIs in Karnataka is considered as the central and dynamic force for the economy and despite their considerable progress in the field of employment generation, it is not free from problems. The problems faced by SSIs are multi-dimensional. According to special group report on difficulties of SSIs in getting finance assistance, delay in the implementation of the project, expensive mode of transport and communication, marketing constraints, cheap low quality items, delay in payments, technological obsolescence in, imperfect knowledge of market condition, lack of infrastructure facilities, deficient managerial and technical skills etc are some of the principal problems encountering the SSIs in the regime of EL. Due to these problems, mortality rate and growth of sick unit in the SSI sector are on increase. The problems of SSIs are many and varied.

Conclusion

SSIs play a dynamic role in the industrial and economic growth of Karnataka. Variety and range of products manufactured by SSIs in Karnataka reflect the progress made in the sector. The achievements of SSIs in the field of job creation, spatial diversification of industrial development, removal of economic disparities among cross sections of people in the economy, utilization of locally available resources, creation of new generation of entrepreneurs, earnings of foreign exchange resources have been noteworthy.

Under the changing globalized, liberalized and privatized business scenario, SSIs have both challenges and opportunities. SSIs can meet the challenges with determination, innovation and hardwork. But it is not so easy task that there is a legacy of restrictions hampering them. Infrastructure bottlenecks and logistic problems are not completely solved in the backward areas. In order to promote SSIs even in the regime of EL measures have been taken by the Government of India and Karnataka in their industrial policy resolutions/statements.

Reference

1. Government of Karnataka (2005), Directorate of Industries and Commerce, Government of Karnataka, *Annual Report year ending 2005-06, (Bangalore: Government of Karnataka)*
2. D'Souza C.M. (2001), "Integrating Environmental Management in Small Industries of India", *Issue 14, (Spring 2001 – Earthday. Electronic Green Journal)*

3. SIDO (2005), Small Industries Development Organization, *Ministry of SSIs Government of India.(New Delhi: Ministry of SSIs Government of India) (Source; SSI Ministry and commerce 2000 Delhi)*
4. OECD (2005), "OECD SME and Entrepreneurship outlook, Defining SMEs", *(France: OECD Publishing) P. 1.1*
5. Bhattacharyya H.K. (1982), "Changing Concept of Small Scale Industries in India", *16-30 April VOL-1 XXVI-7 Yojana(New Delhi: Published by the Director, Publishing Division, Patiala House) Pp. 6-8*
6. Gupta N.S. and Singh Amarith, Industrial Economy of India, *Op.cit., P. 166*
7. Government of India (2000&2005), "SSI in India the Growth Sector for the Millennium, *Present Definitions (w.e.f.24.12.1999) Development Commissioner,SSIs Annual Reports of SIDO for 1992-93 to 2003-04(New Delhi: Small Industries Development Organization, Ministry of SSI's, Government of India)*
8. Vepa.K.Ram(1983), Small Scale Industry, Development and Challenges in Eighties, *(New Delhi:Vikas Publishing House) P. 124*
9. Government of Karnataka [1982] "Small- Scale Industries Government of Karnataka" *State Gazettee Part-1, (Bangalore: Government of Karnataka publication) Pp 821-822).*
10. Gupta Vinod Er (1999), "Types of Enterprises", *October December, (New Delhi: Laghu Udyog Samachar), P. 33-37*
11. Munshi M.C. (1973), "Location of Industry", *in Vakil c.n.(ed), Industrial Development of India- Policy and Problems, kamal Nayan Bajaj Commemoration volume, orient Longman, Bombay, November, P. 250*
12. Raman, V.R.(1993), "The Shape of Things to Come", *Deccan Herald, July 19, P.1*
13. Business standard(2003), "Downfall into the SSI" *Business standard fiscal daily news paper, September 15th, (Bengaluru: Prajavani Press Publishers)*
14. Nangia Ramesh (1979), "Small Scale Industries Development Strategy and Marketing Problems", *Sedme Vol- VI (3), September, (Hyderabad: NISIET) Pp. 217-220*

CHAPTER 7

Entrepreneurship in a Globalising Economy

In recent years rapid globalization has intensified competitive pressure on India's productive activity particularly in the small and medium enterprises. The impact of globalization exposed the SME's for new multi dimensional problems and challenges both in the domestic as well foreign markets. These problems and challenges are to be properly sorted out to maintain the on-going of the SMEs in the country. This needs an army of entrepreneurs equipped with scientific and technological knowledge supported by common sense and vision. There were days believed in the saying that "Entrepreneurs are born not trained", but this cannot be accepted in its totality. The present day opinion is that the entrepreneurial capabilities though inborn, they are to be pulled out and polished by proper training to meet the needs of the present economic situation. This proper solely concentrates on this issue.

Before going in to the different aspects of Entrepreneurship, it is necessary to note the distinction between generally used two terms "Entrepreneur and Entrepreneurship". Entrepreneur and Entrepreneurship are like the two faces of the same coin. The literature on this subject throws a clear light on the meaning of these two terms mention a few.Chronologically the word "Entrepreneur" first appeared in French literally meant "go-between' or "between-taker". In the middle ages, the term was used to refer both an actor and individual overseeing large projects. Later in the 16th century and 17th century it referred to men engaged in military exceptions and civil engineering activities, in the 18th century Cantillen. R. defined this term as a person or dealer also who buys factors and services at certain prices and sells them at uncertain prices in the future.

The Collins could English language dictionary –1987 defined "An entrepreneur is a person who sets up business deals in order to make profit'.J.B. Say says – "An entrepreneur is the economic agent who units all means of production." As the dimensions of the economic activity underwent changes people started looking at the entrepreneurs was widened. This appears to be true if we consider source definitions advanced by some authors. In this context, J.A. Schumpeter is of the view that "A person who introduces innovative changes is an entrepreneur and he is an integral part of economic growth". According to Webster "Entrepreneur is one who assumes risk and management of business." Prof. Walken defined "True entrepreneur is one who is endowed with more than overage capacities in the risk of organizing and co-ordinating various factors of production." In the words of peter Drucker – "Entrepreneur is one who always searches for change, responds to it and exploits it as an opportunity. Innovation is a specific tool of entrepreneurs, the means by which they exploit change as an opportunity for different business or service". A clear understanding of all these definitions portray an entrepreneur as an initiator of action, stimulators of social economic change and harnesses of resources ultimately an individual or a person.

The central of all the definitions may be put in nutshell as that anybody can become an entrepreneur provided he has got a certain set of behavioral traits and mental attitude. His success depends largely on his intelligence, imagination, capacity to innovate and his ability to turn missions in to realities. Hence a successful entrepreneur must have the characteristic features such as hard work, business acumen and sincerity, produce achievement motivation, self-reliance and independence, highly optimistic, keen foresight, planning and organizing ability, innovativeness, risk taking secrecy maintains, maintenance of public relations, communication skill.

By the above it is clear an Entrepreneur is not a Manager- a paid servant entrusted with managerial functions, acts at the directions of the entrepreneur. In recent years a new brand of corporate entrepreneurs called "entrepreneurs" has come into picture, since they average with in the frontiers of an existing enterprise, they are called entrepreneurs. In this "in" refers to "within". In big organizations, the top executives with entrepreneurial talents are encouraged to generate new ideas and then convert then in to products through research and development carried out with in the organization itself. This is necessary to avoid stagnation and decline in his enterprise. This concept of entrepreneurship has gained much popularity in developed countries like America. If the managements are not receptive to their new ideas, they tend to leave their parent organization and start ventures of their own, some times which cause a threat to their parent organization. For this Steve Woznaik working at Hewlett Packard joined with Steve jobs and formed Apple computers. Hence it is highly a welcome gesture that companies should provide entrepreneurs with adequate financial resources and freedom so that their new and innovative ideas can be developed, and realized, which truly helps the economic growth. Here we must note that the entrepreneur differs from the "intreprenuer" with regard to certain aspects. Always an "Entrepreneur" is – independent, He need not be a highly educated, responsibility has to be taken to raise funds for the company, He has to bear risk, He is move concerned with routine work, He operates from out side and more authoritarian Where as an "intereprenuer" is a dependent and cannot decisions himself, He is highly educated and does not have the responsibility of fund raising. He doesn't bear risk, He is a special in his chosen fields, He is a part and parcel of his concern and less authoritarian.

This exercise helps us to understand the difference between the two terms "Entrepreneurs" and "Entrepreneurship". It may be entrepreneur or inetreprener both refer to a person are an individual. Where as "entrepreneurship" refers to the function. To be more clear "entrepreneurs" is a business leader like (a captain of a ship) and the functions performed by him in relation to that businesses entrepreneurship. Thus entrepreneurship refers to a process of action an entrepreneur undertakes to establish his/her enterprise. It is a creative and innovative response to the environment. It is thus a cycle of action to further the interests of the entrepreneur.

In the words of A.H. Cole- "Entrepreneurship is the purposeful activity of an individual or a group of associated individuals, undertaken to imitate, maintain or organize a profit oriented business unit for the production or distribution of economic goods and services". As pointed out by Benjawin Higgins " Entrepreneurship means the function of foreseeing investment and production opportunity, organizing an enterprise to under take new production process, raising capital, hiring labour, arranging for the supply of raw-materials and selecting top managers for the day–to–day operation of the enterprise". According to Schumpeter "Entrepreneurship is bused on purposeful and systematic innovation".

By the above, it is clear that entrepreneurship is a process involving various functions to be undertaken to establish an enterprise and push it through the time successfully. This helps us to identify a few characteristics of entrepreneurship. Such as- Innovation, Risk-bearing, Decision making, Acceptance of challenges, Handling of economic uncertainly, Problem solving systematic Planning, Organization and Management Opportunity seeking. However out of all these innovation and risk bearing are considered to be the basic elements of entrepreneurship.

In the changed context of the economic scenario, needs more emphasis on the development of entrepreneurship. It is essential of only for the survival but also for the festering the economic growth. Increasing army of unemployed Youths. Widening Economic disparities, increasing gap between urban and rural areas in infrastruructure facilities, socio–economic disparities demands for harnessing the resources available for the realization of higher production in all sectors in the country. The exposure of the economy for the Global market forces on the other, needs the strengthening of all the productive sectors of the economy at the earliest. This is possible only by a band of enthusiastic and committed entrepreneurs. For this, the economy needs suitable and effective entrepreneurship development programmes. The entrepreneurship development institutions have to switch over to a more specialized role for training individual entrepreneur of for developing equipping a team of entrepreneurs to take up ventures in groups in specialized product lines, while pursuing entrepreneurship development, it is not enough to think of only promoting an enterprise. Sustainability and growth over a period of time is also equally important. Entrepreneurial development is an organized and systematic development. It is regarded at a tool of industrialization and a solution to employment problems. The process of entrepreneurship development involves – equipping a person with information used for enterprise building, sharpening his entrepreneurial skills, and building the entrepreneurial attitude. Entrepreneurship development is a policy matter for the Government. It is essentially an educational process and an endeavors inhuman resource development. Stepanek identifies certain prerequisites for entrepreneurship development, such as Intelligence, Motivation, Knowledge and Opportunity.

Let us looking to the available possibilities of entrepreneurship development in India, before thinking of new ideas and the organizational set-up in operation in some developed countries in the world. Entrepreneurial talent existed in every country like wise the handicraft entrepreneurship in India was as old as human civilization itself. Indian crafts enjoyed worldwide reputation. This industry flourished till the end of 18th century.

Changes in the Indian Economy took place with the entry of East India Company. Manufacturing entrepreneurship emerged in the country in the second half of the 19th century. Many textile mills came up in Bombay and Ahmedabad. The first steel industry came to be established by J.R.D. Tata in 1911. In the first four decades of the 20th century many manufacturing units were established mainly due to the discriminating protection policy pursued by the Indian Government. The Swadeshi movement gave a much needed fill up to indigenous entrepreneurship. The emergence of Managing Agency system in 1936 also contributed to Indian entrepreneurship.

After Independence the Government of India announced its First Industrial policy in 1948, latest in its successive Industrial policies, the tempo of Industrialization spread entrepreneurship to a wider sphear. The I & II five year plans emphasized the expansion of Industrialization in the Country .The Third five year plan by creating a favorable atmosphere, the small-scale industries spread to rural and small town also. The Vth in Five year plan emphasized the promotion of Entrepreneurship, promotion of consultancy service and incentives were giving to engineers to attract them to this sector. During the VIth in plan measures were taken to promote S.M.Es. The industrial policy statement, 1980, suggested certain steps to provide appropriate training and package to S.M.Es. This entrepreneurship development was given importance. The real efforts were made in1991 industrial policy. Entrepreneur Development progammes were proposed to be built in to the curricula of vocational and other Degree level courses. This policy emphasized the importance of private initiative and entrepreneurship in Industrial development. Realizing the importance of entrepreneurship development the planners and policy makers formulated entrepreneurship Development Programmes.

To make the E.D.P more effective several organizations were established. They are:

1 The Entrepreneurship Development Institute of India was set up in March 1983 at Ahmedabad Jointly by financial Institutions and the Gujarat Government.
2 The National Institute for Entrepreneurship and Small Business Develcpment was established by the Central Government in the year 1983 itself, with the objective of coordinating the activities related to entrepreneurship and small business.
3 Rural entrepreneurship developments Institute at Ranchi came to be established in the year 1983 with a goal to train the entrepreneurs for rural small & medium enterprises.

In addition to these State Bank of India, Public Sector banks Industrial Development Bank of India, State Financial corporations Small Industries Extension Training Institute, District Industries centers are the other organizations activity engaged in conducting entrepreneurship development. Some State Governments too have established center for entrepreneur development in their respective sates. Apart from this a number of universities and Management Institutes have included entrepreneurship in their curriculum.Entrepreneurship development is a complex phenomenon. There is no single model identified as a bench mark for entrepreneurship education and training and it is not clear how entrepreneurship should be introduced. The United States, which a relatively long history in this field has tended to, teach young people how to start their own business. Younger over are taught self-employment as an alternative carried as well as the positive effects of entrepreneurship.

Where as Sweden has launched three year national programmed for entrepreneurship. Finland too has adopted this type of approach aiming as developing an attitude of "intrepreneurship" involving flexibility, creativity, capability of taking risks and initiative – Finland's entrepreneurship project gave raise to a new for reaching curriculum, starting in 2004 requiring primary schools to incorporate and including a thematic entity " Participating citizenship and entrepreneurship" for upper secondary schools. In the U.K. a five year strategy for children and learners is committed to establishing enterprise activity in the school curriculum in secondary schools and to forge closer links between schools and business. Government funded the enterprise education. A enterprise education "entitlement" will provide all key state 4 pupils (14- with the equivalent of five days enterprise activity- (such as running a real, or realistic business). Which builds on existing work related activities like work experience and business mentoring and develops knowledge skills and attitudes for enterprise capability and economic and business understanding. Dutch Government too introduced entrepreneurship education from the school level itself Austria launched the imitative for "teaching entrepreneurship" together with the National Foundation for teaching entrepreneurship in New York, to develop an entirely new programmed for Austrian schools. Hungry, Norway out Spain have incorporated economic and entrepreneurship skill in to the curriculum at school level. Italy has recently introduced a regulation for a flexible school work alternative schedule applying to some secondary level pupils and which can include the use of stimulated enterprises.

In unites states more than 1500 colleges and universities offer some form of entrepreneurship training. Subjects like entrepreneurial finance, family business high technology business, franchising mature business and corporate entrepreneurship at the university level. Several studies show large positive effects on entrepreneurship programmes carried out in the unites states. The Stanford model for entrepreneurship is viewed by many as the Indian driver of sliconvalley of his country. In addition, many other countries are also being show as examples in this direction. This clearly points out that entrepreneurship development comprises of teaching required skill developing activity. It is not merely teaching centered.

It is a purposeful teaching – activity centered training. It is not merely a teaching with in the four walls. The entrepreneurial development must involve teaching of multi disciplines assisted by problem centered discussions, involving experienced expert faculty members, members from financial institutions, marketing experts. Advertising and public relation personnel of leading enterprises. Visiting enterprises and interactions with entrepreneurs and labourers is also essential. The officers of the department of industry should also be involved in this process of entrepreneurship development. After a several visit and participation in some of he Entrepreneurial Development Programmes the effectiveness on the participants is not so positive. The majority of the participants (trainees) attend the programme only with an intention of qualifying themselves for the loans and incentives or subsidies. Even the curriculum does of cover what is required for the up-coming entrepreneurs. Particularly the EDPs at the District Industries Centers level conducted by Government clearly appeals to be for P.M.R.Y facilities. The member who guides say the faculty members as this level will not take the programme seriously and in many cases themselves are not equipped for the purpose. Some private organizations too are being given financial aid to conduct these programmes. In certain cases, these organizations are not service motivated and their aim is only to get money from the Government. Hence it is necessary to supervise and evaluate the work carried out by the department/agency.

Universities must frame the necessary curriculum for the entrepreneurial development. Separate Institutions one to be established for the effective implementation. Faculty by drawn from different sections as the curriculum needs on contract basis for a specific period. Permanency will certainly make them lethargic. In addition, it is at most necessity that the Department/ Government should look at the entrepreneur particularly in case of SMEs with soft corner not only with an intention of exploitation. The financial institutions tool should have positive out look other wise entrepreneurial progammes whatever effective and efficient will to yield the expected results in these days of Globalization and Liberalization.

References

1. Beaverton, Oregon (2005), Initiative Explores Leadership, Management and Innovation. http.www.yahoo.com, March 2006, PP, 1-2.

2. Nagavya(2005), Entrepreneurship Development: Role of Steps, and Innovation and Business Incubation Centre published by Alu House, New Delhi-110002.
3. Potter Jonathan (2005), Local Innovation Systems and SME Innovation Policy, OECD Publishing France P. 13.
4. Gordon E. Natarajan K (2005), "Entrepreneurship Development" Himalaya Publishing House, Hyderabad.
5. Schlogl Herwig (2005), The Role of SMEs and Entrepreneurial Development" Himalaya Publishing Bangalore.
6. Murthy C.S.V.(2004), " Small Scale Industries and Entrepreneurial Development" Himalaya Publishing House Bangalore.
7. Rohling Kerstin and Multhaup Thomas (2005), Innovative SMEs in Germany, OECD Publishing France P.13.
8. Dr.Neeta Baporikar(2002), "Entrepreneurship and Small Scale Industry", Himalaya Publishing Bangalore.
9. Desai Vasant, (2002), "Small-Scale Industries and Entrepreneurship", Himalaya Publishing Bangalore.
10. Dr. Lowrey Ying(2003), The entrepreneur and entrepreneurship: A Neoclassical Approach Presented at the ASSA Annual Meeting.http:www.yahoo.com.March 2006.PP 1-18
11. Dr. Kaptan S.S.(1987), "Small Enterprises Development Management and Extension Journal Volume fourteenth Nuz NISIET Press Hyderabad.

CHAPTER 8

Imbalance in the Growth of SSIs in Mysore District—The Policy Needs

The Geographical area of Mysore District 6269 sq. km.The Geographical area of the district for the convenience of administration and development has been divided into 7 taluks such as Mysore, Nanjanagud, K.R.Nagar, Hunsur, T.Narasipura, H.D.Kote and Periyapatna. The district principally as Agricultural district. The major crops of the district are both in irrigated and non-irrigated areas are Paddy, Sugarcane, Ragi, Jower, Maize, Mulberry, Groundnut, Cotton, Tobacco, Sunflower and Pulses. The main Horticultural crops are coconut, arecanut and banana. This district has a special place for Silk in the world market. According to 2001 census the population of the district is 25850562. The average rainfall in the district is 1058.1mm. Out of the total area under cultivation 13756 hacters comes under the irrigated area. In addition to these factors, the social structure, the traditional and customary habits of the society too have influenced the industrial growth of the district particularly with reference to Small Scale Industries. On the background of these facts a study of the district industrial growth has been visualized in the successive page. As per the statistics of the Action Plan of 2004-05. The number of SSIs registered in the district stood at 20700. The table below furnishes the number of SSIs in each taluks of the district.

Table 1: Taluk-Wise Classification of SSIs in Mysore District (As on 31st March 2005)

Sl.No	*Taluks*	*No of SSIs*	*Percentage*
01	Mysore	10980	53.04
02	Periyapatna	1181	5.71
03	Nanjangud	2608	12.60
04	K.R.Nagar	1554	7.51

05	Hunsur	1648	7.96
06	T.N.Pura	1541	7.44
07	H.D.Kote	1188	5.74
Total Number of SSIs		20700	100.0

Source: DIC (2005) , Small Scale Industries" , Number of small scale units registered in District Industrial Centre till the end of 31st March 2005, District Industries Centre, Mysore.

Taluk-Wise Classification of Registered SSIs of Mysore District

The table indicates clearly out of the total number of SSIs in the district Mysore taluk has a major place with 10980 units. The percentage being 53.40. It is followed by Nanjangud taluk. A taluk very close to Mysore with 2608 units. The percentage being 12.60. This taluk is followed by followed by Hunsur (7.96%), K.R.Nagar (7.51%), T.N.Pura(7.44%), H.D.Kote (5.74%) and Periyapatna(5.71%). Periyapatna has only 1181 (SSI/Tiny) units. The percentage being 5.71 i.e. the least in the district. This is evident there is a concentration of SSIs/Tiny units. Particularly in Mysore Taluk and the very closer taluk of Nanjanagud.

This situation of concentration still appears to be more if we take into consideration the category-wise distribution of SSIs in the district. The table No. 2 indicates the category-wise classification of registered SSIs/Tiny of the district.

Table 2: Category-Wise Classification Number of Registered SSIs of Mysore District (As on 31st March 2005)

Sl.No	*Category*	*Number of SSIs*	*Percentage*
1	Food	3229	15.60
2	Textiles	3269	15.79
3	Engineering	1966	9.50
4	Wood	3228	15.59
5	Electrical and Electronics	446	2.15
6	Chemicals	1122	5.42
7	Rubber and Plastics	499	2.41
8	Paper and printing	501	2.42
9	Job works/Repairs/services	907	4.38

10	Leather	597	2.88
11	Glass and Ceramics	584	2.82
12	Automobiles	56	0.27
13	Ferrous and Nonferrous	04	0.02
14	Others	4292	20.73
	Total No of SSIs	20700	100.0

Source: DIC (2005), Action Pl an 2004-05, N umber of small scale units registered in District Industrial Centre till the end of 31st March 2005, District Industries Centre, Mysore(Mysore: District Industries Centre)

Category-Wise Classification Number of Registered SSIs of Mysore District

Of the total 20700 SSIs in the district 20.73% belong to 14th category i.e., others category. Textiles units constituting (15.79%) occupied the second place in the district. Food (15.60%), Wood (15.59%), Engineering (9.50%), Chemicals (5.42%), Job works/ Repairs/Services (4.38%) occupied the third, fourth, fifth, sixth and seventh places respectively. The next successive places are occupied by Leather (2.88%), Glass and Ceramics (2.82%), Paper and Printing (2.42%), Rubber and Plastics (2.41%), Electrical and Electronics (2.15%). Automobiles, Ferrous and Nonferrous units respectively occupied the last places.

The category-wise distribution too exhibits the same trend in the growth of SSI/Tiny units in the district. The table below points out this in a very clear way.

Table 3: Industry Group-wise No. of Registered SSIs of Mysore District (Up to 2004-05) Mysore Taluk: Urban

Sl	*Taluk*	*Food*	*Textiles*	*Engineering*	*Wood*	*Electrical and Electronics*	*Chemicals*	*Rubber and Plastics*	*Paper and Printing*	*Job works/ repairs/ services*	*Leather and its Products*	*Glass and Ceramics*	*Auto mobile*	*Ferrous and Nonferrous*	*Others*	*Total units*	*Total workers*
1	Mysore	1808	2030	1150	1537	276	495	417	412	368	389	421	56	4	1617	10980	67021
	Total	**1808**	**2030**	**1150**	**1537**	**276**	**495**	**417**	**412**	**368**	**389**	**421**	**56**	**4**	**1617**	**10980**	**67021**

Source: DIC (2005) , Small Scale Industries" , No. of small scale units registered in District Industrial Centre till the end of 31st March 2005, District Industries Centre, Mysore.

Table 4: Industries Group-wise No. of Registered SSIs of Mysore District (Up to 2004-05) Rural

Sl No.	*Taluk*	*Food*	*Textiles*	*Engineering*	*Wood*	*Electrical and Electronics*	*Chemicals*	*Rubber and Plastics*	*Paper and Printing*	*Job works/ repairs/ services*	*Leather and its Products*	*Glass and Ceramics*	*Auto mobile*	*Ferrous and Nonferrous*	*Others*	*Total units*	*Total workers*
1	Periyapatna	218	212	120	256	14	77	9	9	61	36	17	0	0	152	1181	5141
2	Nanjangud	378	289	255	324	28	222	36	36	144	58	45	0	0	793	2608	8301
3	K.R.Nagar	214	126	90	238	12	77	9	15	87	27	26	0	0	633	1554	5615
4	Hunsur	210	220	192	345	99	85	10	12	124	26	38	0	0	287	1648	5599
5	T.N.Pura	218	216	134	331	15	96	11	11	71	53	21	0	0	364	1541	4621
6	H.D.Kote	183	176	25	197	02	70	7	6	52	08	16	0	0	446	1188	3928
	Total	1421	1239	816	1691	170	627	82	89	539	208	163	0	0	2675	9720	33205
	Grand total	3229	3269	1966	3228	446	1122	499	501	907	597	584	56	4	4292	19177	100226

Source: DIC (2005), Small Scale Industries", No. of small scale units registered in District Industrial Centre till the end of 31st March 2005, District Industries Centre, Mysore.

Even here Mysore taluk and Nanjanagud taluk exhibits a clear cut concentration of SSI/Tiny units in most of the categories.

It is evident also with reference to the capital investment and the volume of employment. It has been shown in the tale below:

Table 5: Profile of the Units ,Investment and Employment in Mysore District: (Urban and the Rural in Mysore District i.e., from 1991-92 to 2004-05)

Year	Urban Mysore Unit	Investment	Rural P.Patna Employment	Units	Investment	Employment	N.Gud Unit	Investment	Employment	K.R.Nagar Unit	Investment	Employment
1991-92	270	619.42	1874	53	68.13	206	45	113.5	353	61	8.01	155
1992-93	193	316.11	1049	18	18.44	51	12	29.33	62	3	4.13	15
1993-94	226	525.34	1358	60	13.89	171	39	47.06	209	58	12.26	122
1994-95	229	825.64	1595	49	24.5	123	25	42.58	120	46	18.57	114
1995-96	307	1687.2	1863	18	32.08	66	20	88.6	194	26	18.7	66
1996-97	283	512.55	1580	30	20.55	98	17	156.5	104	20	12.78	60
1997-98	355	980.63	2047	84	324.8	174	221	451.1	668	150	13	291
1998-99	161	515.5	886	9	84.62	96	62	121.9	99	9	28.53	72
1999-00	210	590.1	906	10	41.12	47	63	105.8	256	17	24.94	57
2000-01	496	1015	1523	97	315.6	612	121	489.3	815	58	289.6	256
2001-02	610	1315.6	1839	89	245	542	101	326.6	652	64	126	125

2002-03	145	584.56	1000	65	68.59	230	110	89	110	28	115.9	101
2003-04	115	158.89	512	56	89.58	110	89	138	416	48	89.57	215
2004-05	158	1685.2	1056	55	14.05	59	85	173.3	199	64	34.95	102
Total	3758	11332	19088	693	1361	2585	1010	2373	4257	652	796.9	1751

Year	*Rural Units*	*Inves ments*	*Employ ment*	*Units*	*Invest ments*	*Employ ment*	*Units*	*Invest ment*	*Employ ment*
1991-92	56	28.96	252	85	61.96	317	49	8.21	131
1992-93	18	17.09	91	19	57.15	80	43	3.02	102
1993-94	53	14.82	128	15	24.31	80	56	18.38	163
1994-95	21	26.96	52	18	64.14	92	29	31.75	58
1995-96	21	25.58	63	18	68.3	84	4	18.54	25
1996-97	38	48.6	138	76	75.22	211	50	24.8	99
1997-98	155	102	390	121	97.55	390	91	128.25	311
1998-99	23	84.98	198	14	40.84	83	10	52.5	106
1999-00	33	36.38	100	16	15.2	53	9	18.59	2
2000-01	99	187.89	454	110	401.4	458	71	200.2	463
2001-02	87	160	189	86	112.9	65	63	127.06	72
2002-03	89	197	149	56	199.6	151	56	300.37	149
2003-04	87	115.89	312	100	315.3	68	100	171.82	151
2004-05	55	54.39	96	15	5.08	28	43	35	81
Total	835	1100.5	2612	749	1539	2160	674	1138.5	1913

Source: DIC (2005), Small Scale Industries", No. of small scale units registered in District Industrial Centre till the end of 31st March 2005, District Industries Centre, Mysore.

The statistics provided in the tables above in general the exhibits that there is a total concentration of SSIs/Tiny units is found in the Mysore Taluk. And it's near by place which may be categorized as an urban area. The other taluk have very less density with regard to the SSI/Tiny units. Thus very easy for one to generalize that there is an imbalanced growth of SSIs/Tiny industries in the district. This sort of imbalanced growth is caused by certain factors such as, the infrastructural development in and around Mysore taluk. The facilities created by KIADB, the facilities provided by the KSSIDC, the existence of GTTC and other Consultative organizations, and Administrative convenience by DIC, the existence of Banking organizations, availability of Trained, Skilled labour force etc.It is evident this sort of imbalanced growth in a way promoted rural population (rural taluks i.e. Hunsur, K.R.Nagar, H.D.Kote, Nanjanagud, Periyapatna and T.Narasipura) to migrate to the urban taluk i.e. Mysore which indirectly hampers the agricultural activities in those taluks. This ultimately forms a big bottleneck for the total economic growth of the district.

It is high time to think of remedial measures for this over concentration of SSIs/Tiny units

Measures

To overcome the overconcentration of SSIs a few measures may be contemplated apart. A few may be :

1. The SSIs which desires to move in to the rural areas and those investor's whishes to establish SSIs in rural areas are to be provided with additional and extra amenities compare to be the SSI units of the district headquarters. In the form of subsides, grants, land, easy supply of power& water, and financial facilities at a lower rate of interest.
2. It is really high time to develop industrial estates and a network of plots at rural areas to be provided to the upcoming SSIs.
3. Technical knowhow be provided to the SSI unit which comes up in rural areas at their doorsteps.
4. The marketing facilities are provided by establishing an organization to take up the responsibility.
5. A suitable classification (referred table.4) of SSIs be made,

on the basis of available of raw materials, in the rural areas for particular SSIs and such once be encouraged only in rural areas. Such of the units are mostly in the agro based and forest based. They are not being given place in urban areas or such once been discouraged to be established in urban areas.

6. A suitable industrial policy to be enacted to reserve such productive activities only to SSIs of rural areas. The major industries are to be discouraged to produce such products reserve for SSIs.
7. In cases of transportation of finished products and raw materials, taxes or any levies on units of rural area are exempted.
8. Strengthening of and establishment of SSIs in rural areas on the one hand, helps generation of rural employment meeting, it's the problem of migration rural to urban and strengthen the agricultural population economically .In a way in the rural areas agricultural as well industry go hand in hand uplifting the rural society economically as well social.

Reference

Jeevan Reddy B.P.(2002), " Patents and Trade Marks: Impact on Small Scale and Medium Scale Industries", sedme, Vol. 29(1), NISIET Hyderabad: 1-3.

.Raju S.V. (20010, "The recent environmental Changes and Impact on Small Scale Industrial Sector", Southern Economist, April, Bangalore. 7-9.

.Godbole, M.D. (1978), Industrial Dispersal Policies, Himalya Publishing House, Bombay, 1.

.Veerasekharappa and Varsudeva Rao D. (1985), "Karnataka Economy a Speical

Survey, Regional Development and Industrilisation causes or effect a case study in 8.Karnataka, Southern Economist Journal, November, Vol ( ), Bangalore, 5-6.

.Ibid, Government of India (GOI) (1961), Report of the Committee on Dispersal of Industries, Small Scale Industies Board, Novermber, New Delhi, 6.

Government of India (GOI) (1980), National Committee an the development of Backward Areas, Report on Industrial Dispersal, Planning Commission, October New Delhi, 71.

Government of Karnataka (2001), "New Industrial Policy, 2001-06", Government of Karnataka, Bangalore 7, 18-22.

Government of Karnataka, (G.O.K.), (2004-05) ," Trends of Small Scale Industries Districts Wise Growth SSI units in Karnataka", Directorate of Industries and Commerce, Government of Karnataka, Bangalore.

CHAPTER 9

State Level Economic Reforms —with special Reference to Infrastructure Sector of Karnataka

The progress of economic reforms in India during the last 14 years has been reasonably good but further reforms need to be put in place to ensure higher economic growth rate. Government of India is continuing with the reforms package for industrial sector so as to ensure that the Indian economy achieves the eight percent growth rate in the country. For this, large scale customs and excise rationisation, personal tax reforms, restructuring of the banking sector, policies facilitating greater flow of foreign direct investment, infrastructural development, fastening of reforms at the State level, improvement in the financial health of the states etc., need to give high priority. Industries are geographically situated in the states, and are subject to rules and regulations applied by the states in authorizing the installation of plants and in ensuring that they operate within the framework of existing laws and rules, whereas Union Government has been busy in dismantling controls and changing rules in its own domain. States are advised by the Union Government to speed up reforms at various levels to set right their dismal state of financial health. This paper analyses to concentrate on State Level Economic Reforms with special reference to infrastructure reforms Karnataka.

Pre-Requisites for State Level Reforms

The economic reforms introduced by the Union Government have made sufficient provision for the states to introduce economic reforms at the state level and attract private capital in the fields of power, irrigation, road, parks, and all areas of industry. As rightly stated in World Bank Study Report headed by Zoubida Allaon, it is the ability of the state to attract private capital which determines a states' growth performance. The flows of private capital to a particular state, among others, are depending upon investor–friendly environment (IFE). The IFE encompasses an advanced infrastructure, skilled working class, investor friendly rules and regulations and moderate tax policy. Significant reforms are needed to bring this about in the states of India.

i) Policy, pricing, institutional and regulatory reforms to induce private sector to invest in infrastructure into commercially viable projects and improvements in the capacity of states to manage commercially enforceable contracts;
ii) An environment suitable to efficient public investment in areas where the public sector will remain important such as roads and urban services;
iii) Public expenditure reforms to set aside unnecessary spending, and make room for priority programmes in public infrastructure, health and education; and
iv) Tax reforms to provide stable sources of revenue at a low efficiency cost.

According to World Bank Report, policy, pricing and institutional reforms of key sectors would bring about the needed fiscal restructuring in the states power and irrigation reforms would help to increase fiscal gains in virtually all the states of the country. In states like Maharashtra, Karnataka, Gujrath, policy, pricing and institutional reforms alone, would be sufficient to restore fiscal sustainability. In other states, like Andhra Pradesh, Rajastan, Tamil Nadu, West Bengal, Haryana, putting the states public finances on a sustainable path would require more comprehensive reforms of public expenditures such as public enterprise reforms, freeze on public employment, reduction in consumption subsidies; and for some of the states, a rationalization and retargeting of welfare programmes. In backward states such as Orissa, Bihar and Uttar Pradesh, sectoral reforms and public expenditure restructuring may need to be complemented by debt refinancing.

Infrastructure Policy Reforms at the State Level

In India, PSUs of Union Government and States have

traditionally been responsible for the development of infrastructure facilities. Considerable resources have been invested in telecommunications, power and transport with mixed results. While the industrial sector has been growing rapidly, additions and improvements to infrastructure have been not adequate to keep up with demand. The demand for basic infrastructure has also been followed by the increasing number of foreign investors setting up factories in the country to produce manufactured goods. Infrastructure constraints have also been compounded by poor management and the inefficient pricing of resources.

Most of PSUs involved in infrastructure development do not posses the adequate managerial ability nor economic strength needed to oversee the much – needed expansion of infrastructure. The issue of inadequate infrastructure facilities must be resolved if the country is to achieve the targeted growth rate of eight percent. Government of India and various states have opened up their public utility industries to private sector both domestic and foreign. In the telecommunications industry, the Union Government not only allowed foreign companies to build and operate the telecommunications net work, the companies may even be given the option of renewing their licenses after 15 years, effectively owing the networks in the interim.

The need to overcome the infrastructural bottlenecks is becoming a critical issue for all the states. In the changed global scenario, any delay in the planned infrastructure projects make the states less competitive and might even stunt their economic growth.Regarding commercialization of infrastructural facilities, the progress in the states is not adequate. Hence, Government of India has directed the states to speed up infrastructure reform policies. Several states have already started the implementation of reforms in the infrastructure sector particularly in the fields of power, parks, roads and restructuring of public expenditure and in the revenue front.

Power Sector Reforms

Power sector used to run by State Electricity Board (SEBs). They were responsible for generating and distributing power, setting tariffs and collecting revenue. Due to power theft, social subsidy scheme, transmission losses, accumulation heavy amount of dues and interest, SEBs of majority of states were incurring losses.

In power sector, recognising the fact that SEBs credit worthiness must be restored to attract private capital, Karnataka, Maharashtra, Tamil Nadu, Andhra Pradesh and other states have introduced power sector reforms which enordorse (i) establishment of an independent regulatory agency (ii) tariffs reflecting costs (iii) competition among independent power producers (iv) divestiture of shares in the power generating PSUs and restructuring and privatization of the distribution functions of the SEBs. This approach has laid out in a Common Minimum National Action Plan for Power (CMAP 1996) issued by Union Ministry of Power, on the basis of agreements reached in Chief Ministers Conferences. Steps have been taken to implement tariff reforms in various states which include the following:

1. Higher prices actually collected on electricity use is the first order of business.
2. Privatization of power generation and the conversion of SEBs from power providers to market regulators would come next.
3. Power capacity will not be expanded until the SEBs are fundamentally overhauled or eliminated.
4. Even private power projects were expected to sell their electricity to the SEBs as they were the power purchasers; so that the bank ability of private sector power projects depended fundamentally on the financial health of the SEBs.

Water Supply Reforms

In water, investment for rehabilitation and modernization (RM) along with volume–based pricing and institutional changes would provide the basis for efficient water use, cost recovery and improved service delivery in canal irrigation. The RM of irrigation schemes would restore the reliability of water delivery without which farmers will be reluctant to pay higher water charges.

The RM Irrigation scheme makes provision for the introduction of volume–based pricing of water management practices. Institutional reforms like formation of Water Users' Associations, provide the basis and necessary financial incentives for improved cost recovery as well as improved accountability in the delivery of water services to farmers. Tamil Nadu, Andhra Pradesh and Orissa have started (1997) reforms with the objectives of the cost recovery, quality of service delivery to farmers, and systems turn over to water users. In its 1995 agricultural policy Karnataka state proposed radically to transform institutional incentives in the irrigation sector. Even through there is wider scope for private participation in urban water supply some reform–minded municipalities have been nonetheless successful in attracting private capital and expertise.

PWD Reforms

Reforming the Public Works Departments removes main obstacle to efficient road construction. To overcome the capacity constraints of PWDs, private professional engineering firms have to be contracted to investigate and design large costly sections of road suitable for construction by machine intensive methods alone. The World Bank Team has suggested for downsizing and retraining of in-house PWD engineering staff. This means a smaller but very important role for State PWDs as planner, administrator and maintainer of roads. The professional engineering firms investigates and design roads, supervise construction and maintenance and supply material and equipment. The PWD reforms are implemented in various states and roads are being constructed on international standards.

Reforms of Ports

Ports of India face capacity shortages and low productivity levels. Government of India has implemented several measures for improving the institutional framework and induces private investment to ports. Maritime States have implemented similar reforms to develop their ports and relieve major ports. Some states have identified projects worth $ one billion to develop their medium ports. However, according to World Bank Team, despite the attractiveness of such investments to the private sector, they are considered a complement to, but not a full substitute for, investments by the states or individual port trusts.

Urban Reforms

Towns and Cities (TCs) are facing under investment and shortages of key services. The problems of TCs relate to the weak fiscal base–eroded by state law imposing rent controls, limits on the amount of land an individual can hold, restrictions on land markets, and unrealistically low water rates. In some of TCs, revenues are excessively dependent on inefficient taxes which need to be eliminated. According to the World Bank, the Urban Reforms need the following measures.

a. Improving the use of the existing resource base like better cost recovery and enforcement of existing taxes.
b. Strengthening of the resource base and make it more efficient which include lifting of rent controls in the major cities, eliminating octroi, setting up of efficient land markets with an effective system of land titling and
c. Need for establishing a rule–based, efficient system of capital grants to replace the present system.

These measures help to provide the basis for the restoration of the finances of the urban areas and thus restore their capacity to invest in critically needed infrastructure. These measures would also help urban governments become credit worthy borrowers, able to access capital markets and raise funds for critically needed investments. Already, various states have introduced some of these measures, by providing access to capital markets and in turn these measures have provided incentives for urban governments to improve their financial management.

Infrastructure Reforms in Karnataka

Karnataka, one of the country's fastest growing states, and an icon of liberalization, exhibits some typical characteristics of a reforming economy. It was the only state to have experienced a growth rate of eight percent in the second half of 1990s. It has undertaken a series of economic reforms which have been supported by a World Bank Assistance package (Rs.12000 crore) to cover six major projects. These include restructuring plan of Rs.5000 crore for a period of four years (2002 – 06). This plan covers power sector reforms, public expenditure reforms, transition to VAT and governance reforms. Others in the aid package are the state high ways, water shed management, rural water supply and management and desiltation of tanks. Also, the World Bank has approved a $ 216 million (2006) loan to the State to fund the delivery of urban services through enhancing infrastructure and improving the institutional and financial frame works at the state and local levels.

Karnataka has undertaken several procedural and policy reforms for the development of infrastructure in the state. The thrust of the infrastructure policy reform of Karnataka is on building up of infrastructure in areas such as power generation, express high ways, industrial parks, townships, Air ports and ports with active participation of private sector. The industrial reforms of the state intends to replace the 'Bureaucratic Approach' with an advanced 'Professional Outlook'. More specifically, industrial reforms can be enumenated as given below:

1. Simplification of rules and regulations concerning the development infrastructural facilities
2. Making provision for the private participation in the field of infrastructure development.
3. Permission for the conversion of land into non–agricultural use such.
4. Policy on spatial diversification in infrastructural development.
5. Expediting the decision making process for the non–resident Indians and Foreign direct investment (NRI and FDI)
6. Opening up of Single Window Agency for speedy clearing of infrastructural projects.
7. Measures of providing of better quality of services, power, infrastructural facilities and improvement in the quality of higher education and training.
8. Liberalisation of inter–state barriers, check posts, collection points on national highways or what ever.
9. Tax Reforms

Karnataka has designated nodal agencies under the Directorate of Industries and Commerce to promote industrial investment in the State. Karnataka Udyog Mitra acts as the single window clearing agency and offers escort services for proposals under Rs.50 Crore, the Karnataka Industrial Areas Development Board acquires land, develops, and allots to the entrepreneurs for establishing industrial units..

To tide over the major problem of inadequate infrastructure – power, water and road – the Government is wooing investors in these high priority areas and a Mega Infrastructure programme is launched in the state. The joint venture Bangalore International Air Port Project at Devanahally, the private promoted Bangalore–Mysore Toll Express Way and Infrastructure Corridor; upgradation of the minor Air ports; development of minor Sea ports, and a World Bank funded upgradation of state highways are all part of this mega agenda.

Active as a show piece of all these impressive achievements is Bangalore, which earned a firm foot hold in the world technology map through its hugely successful strides in software development. For the record, the technology – driven city is adjudged as one of the ten hottest tech cities of the world by famous international business periodicals – News Week and Business Week.

Power Sector Reforms

In August 1999, the Karnataka Electricity Reforms Bill was enacted. The Karnataka Electricity Board is corporatised into the Karnataka Power Transmission Corporation Ltd. (KPTCL) and more importantly the Karnataka Electricity Regulatory Commission is established. The State Government has invited private sector participation in the distribution of electricity in the state. Government intends to attempt privatisation of all companies simultaneously and complete the process in a period of two years.

The State Government has unbundled the distribution function of KPTCL and four independent state owned electricity supply companies (ESCOMS) have been formed on regional basis viz., Bangalore Electricity Supply Company (BESCOM), Hubli Electricity Supply Company (HESCOM), Mangalore Electricity

Supply Company (MESCOM) and Gulbarga Electricity Supply Company (GESCOM). These companies are assigned distribution and retail supply license of KPTCL after getting approval from KERC. In tune with the state policy, these companies are taking several reforms to improve the quality of power supply to consumers, establish proper system of energy accounting, metering and recovery.

Table 1: Generation, Imports, T and D Losses and Consumption of Power in Karnataka

Year	*Power Generation installed capacity (MSW)*	*Electricity Generation (million units)*	*Imports (million units)*	*T and D losses (%)*	*Power consumption (million units)*
1999 – 2000	4423.87	21092	6056	38.00	16151
2000 – 2001	4525.14	21119	6621	35.50	17867
2001 – 2002	4411.54	19214	7609	35.86	18639
2002 – 2003	4699.03	18105	9043	30.70	19888
2003 – 2004	4719.83	19086	10220	29.76	21930
2004 – 2005	4884.83	20462	9380	29.78	23341

Source: Government of Karnataka (2005) Economic Survey 2004 – 05 (Bangalore : Planning and Statistics Department)
* Excluding private sector

The state Government has announced implementation of three years metering programme to complete metering all unmetred consumers and to set up full scale energy audit. Accordingly, a policy direction has issued to change the IP set consumers as per actual energy consumed or at HP rates which ever is lower. This measure is intended to increase the acceptability and accelerate universal metering programme. All the ESCOMS are taking steps to implement this programme.

The state has come out with its revised independent power producers policy with a clearly delineated "no Escrow" stance. Escrow cover relates to the financial security package an IPP demands from the Government for producing power.

Over 16 lakhs beneficiaries under the Bhagyajyothi and Kuteera Jyothi schemes would be given only 18 units of free electricity per month henceforth. The state has also decided to waive off Rs.157 crore arrears from these beneficiaries following unrestricted power supply. It is also decided in the state to regularize 1.35 lakh un-authorised pumsets owned by people and allow them to install metres by paying yearly minimum deposit of Rs.10000 and Rs.2000 towards installment charges.

Road Reforms

Karnataka has launched massive road construction programme. One of the major initiatives is the World Bank assisted High Ways Improvement Project, which covers, 2,263 kms of roads. In this high ways sector, five major schemes have been sanctioned and they are:

1. Golden quadrilateral scheme covering 625 kms at a cost of Rs.320 crores.
2. The new National Highway NH 218 announced by the Union Government
3. North–South and East–West Corridor connecting Kashmir and Kanyakumari and Silchar to Saurashtra respectively.
4. The Central Road Fund Scheme, which is only extended to national high ways covers state high ways and major district roads.
5. Cable–stayed bridge over the railway line of Krishnarajapuram at a cost of Rs.42 crore.

In the state high ways sector, the State Government has taken major initiatives (i) The establishment of the Karnataka Road Development Corporation Ltd., (KRDCL) to moblise resources from financial institutions (ii) the decision of entrusting road maintenance to private agencies.

Table 2: Road Length in Karnataka (in Kms)

Year	*National Highways*	*State Highways*	*Major District Roads*	*All Roads**
1991 – 1992	1997	11288	18063	133987
1992 – 1993	1997	11288	28169	134592
1993 – 1994	1997	11395	28139	134832
1994 – 1995	1997	11395	28284	135104
1995 – 1996	1997	11395	2831	137520
1996 – 1997	1997	11395	28311	137520
1997 – 1998	2355	11037	28361	142801
1998 – 1999	3524	10021	28247	144846

1999 – 2000	3728	9829	28247	148589
2000 – 2001	3728	9829	28247	154204
2001 – 2002	3728	9829	28247	154204
2003 – 2004	3728	2829	28247	154204
2004 – 2005	3967	9590	38247	164164

* National + State Highways, Major District Roads, others District Roads M.unicipal Roads, other Roads

Source: Government of Karnataka (2005) Economic Survey 2004 – 05 (Bangalore: Planning and Statistics Department)

Apart from Central and State high ways, the State Government has also launched massive programme to improve roads in the districts under major districts road programme (MDRP). Karnataka has witnessed major strides in building and maintenance of bridges with HUDCO assistance. The State Government has launched four major projects for improving the Bangalore–Mysore, Mysore–Bantwal, Belur–Belikere and Jewargi–Bijapur ring roads. Work on the State High Ways Maintenance Project is progressing in respect of 7000 km, private sector participation is envisaged for a period of three years in the HUDCO assistance.

The State Government has almost completed a massive scheme of construction of 19 flyovers in Bangalore. Another initiative of Karnataka is the Bangalore–Mysore Infrastructure corridor project taken up by NICEL on BOOT basis (Rs.2000 crores project). This involves construction of an express high way of 111 Kms, Peripheral Roads of over 41 km, Link roads of 9.10 km and elevated roads of 3 kms and development of five Townships. The BMIC will help to reduce the travel time between Bangalore and Mysore from three hours to one hour and 15 minutes.

The Panchayat Raj and Rural Development Department is developing rural roads by investing Rs.92 crores under the PMs Sadak yojana. With these major on going projects and other ambitions proposals, the public works department is poised for a radical transformation.

Metro Rail Project

MRP has been conceived as a joint venture of the State Government and the Union Government along with debt raised from nearly 20 FIs led by UTI Bank. For MRP while state Government will provide Rs.1807 crores, the Union Government would contribute Rs.1447 crores and the FIs the remaining Rs.2953 crores. The first train from Bangalore is expected to run by October 2008.

Bangalore Mass Rapid Transit Ltd. (BMRTL) has been entrusted with the task of planning, designing and land acquisition, any shifting of utilities in the way and short listing of contractors and vendors for the MRP. The land for MRP would include 102 acres from the defence authorities, 55 acres from the State Government and 40 acres from private owners. A 7–KM stretch would be built underground around Vidhana Soudha and the rest would be elevated.

Urban Water Supply Reforms

For this scheme, the World Bank has extended financial assistance of Rs.237.07 crores. Karnataka Urban Infrastructure and Finance Corporation is the nodal agency for this scheme. Under this scheme 24 hours water will be supplied in Municipal Corporation Areas of Belgaum, Gulbarga, Hubli–Dharwad. This is a novel scheme of checking the leakage in the water supply and utilizing locally available water sources. If this scheme is succeeded it will be extended other Urban Centres of the State.

Sanitation Reforms

To make cities lovable and livable, there is need for proper management of city wastes. In Karnataka, the waste management project is taken up jointly with German Cooperation (GIZ) which is providing financial assistance to the tune of Euro 1.5 million. The solid wastes and effluent waters are being treated and bio-manure is produced by private entrepreneurs in cities like Bangalore, Mysore and other places.

Ports Reforms

The ports policy of Karnataka adopted a strategy to use private investment for the creation of port facilities, development of new sites and supporting infrastructure, maritime related industries and coastal shipping and port facilities for power projects. The Karnataka State Industrial Investment and Development Corporation has been appointed as nodal agency for the implementation of this policy. A committee has been constituted to finalise the framework agreement with private companies. Private participation is allowed for three ports namely Belekere, Tadri and Old Mangalore.

Government of India, has announced its decision to go in for joint ventures between major ports and foreign ports, between major and minor ports, and major ports and Indian companies for improvement of port infrastructure. Under this joint venture, a scheme has been formulated for construction of additional berths at Karwar port to meet the anticipated Cargo growth and sent to New Mangalore Port Trust.

Irrigation Reforms

The cumulative irrigation potential under major, medium and minor irrigation increased to 30.91 lakh hectares in 2003 – 2004 from 29.35 lakhs hectores in 2002 – 2003. Additional potential of 1.56 laksh hectares is created in 2003 – 2004.

Karnataka has announced state water policy in January 2002. The salient features of the policy can be enumerated as given below.

1. Providing drinking water at the rate of 55 litres per person per day in rural areas, 70 litres per persons per day in towns and 100 litres per person per day in the city municipal council areas and 135 litres per person per day in city corporation areas.
2. Creation of an ultimate irrigation potential of 45 lakh hectares. Facilities creation of an additional irrigation potential of 16 lakhs hectares by individual farmers using ground water.
3. Improving performance of all water resources projects.
4. Improving productivity of irrigated agriculture by involving users in irrigation management.
5. Harnessing the hydro potential in the state.
6. Providing a legislative, administrative and infrastructural environment, which will ensure fair, just and equitable

distribution and utilization of the water resources of the state to benefit all the people of the state.

Community Based Tank Management Project

Karnataka has sought the World Bank's permission to utilize saved funds to rejuvenate 700 more tanks under the Rs.678 crore Community Based Tank Management Project. The State hopes to save upto Rs.140 crores from the project, targeted to review 2005 tanks in nine districts by 2008–09. As many as 270 tanks had been rejuvenated till now.

The project has planned to cumulative target to complete the revival of over 600 tanks under the Jala Samvardhana Yojana Project by the end of June 2005. The project promoted the Madagascar method of Paddy cultivation among the beneficiaries for getting more yield with less water. The State Government has recovered 89 hectares of land encroached upon in tank areas and it is planning to bring in a law against encroachment of tanks.

Action Points for the State Governments

The foregoing description is indicative of the action expected from the states in various crucial areas, the important among which can be enumerated as given below:

I. Governance Reforms

Corruption and poor governance are the first and the foremost areas to be set right by the states. There should be proper training and motivation for the Ministers, peoples' representatives and the Bureancrats in the fields of administration, development aspects and values in life. Efficient, and honest administration help to go a long way in achieving economic development of the States. Government of India and the States are borrowing heavy amount of funds from the foreign sources and financial institutions by paying exorbitant rate of interest. This fund should be used in an economic and efficient manner for the building of income giving assets in the country. The states should see that borrowed funds should generate adequate income to facilitate for the repayment to the lenders. This will go a long way in reducing fiscal deficit and increasing growth rate of the states and the country as a whole.

2. Irrigation Sector Reforms

Irrigation sector is very vital for the development of rural areas of the States. The incessant poverty is, among others largely due to lack of irrigation facilities to the farmers. Fund shortage should not come in the way of taking up of irrigation projects. Water resources available in the states should not go waste. The funds borrowed for the irrigation sector should be utilized carefully to complete the projects in the stipulated time to overcome the problem of cost escalation. Proper reforms need to be introduced to recover the cost of development of irrigation projects to facilitate repayment to the lenders. Irrigation projects should be followed by proper forestation, fishery development programmes to create additional sources of income and employment.

3. Power Sector Reforms

Power sector reforms are bit withered in the states due to competitive populism among political parties. In the name of poor, rich are getting the benefit in the field of power. Deeper probe in the matter is needed. Unfortunately, most political parties have drawn wrong message from the 2004 electron result and trying to put the persuit of reforms process on the backburner. This appears to be more so in the case of PSRs, going by the way the State Governments (Andhra Pradesh, Tamil Nadu, Maharashtara to name a few) have been vying with one another in offering free power to farmers, throwing all caution and fiscal prudence to winds. Power may be supplied free of cost to too poor farmers but this must be followed by proper check of power theft by the rich people belonging to different sectors of the economy.

There are also other ill effects of free power to farm sector such as the farmers using obsolete power guzzling pumpsets, not bothering to switch off the pumpsets leading to enormous wastage of water and growing more water using crops like paddy and sugar cane. As a result, the water deposits has been going down at an alarming rate. If the States continues with the practice of supplying free power to any group of consumers, it will not inspire private investors to invest on a massive scale in a sick industry.

Unbundling measures of SEBs are of vital importance not only for inducing private investment but also to deal with the serious problems encountering the power sector such as gross mismanagement, rampant corruption and large scale power thefts. It is open secret that a considerable proportion of the so called transmission and distribution losses are in fact power theft. According to one estimate, India could save $ 12 billion merely by improving efficiency in power generation and removing transmission and distribution bottlenecks, as it will drastically reduce the new capacity requirement.

4. Infrastructure Reforms

Still there is wider scope for private participation in the development of infrastructural facilities. If it is not possible to reduce public sector investment in infrastructure development as pointed out by Rakesh Mohan, the corresponding implication should be that the public sector infrastructure investment will have to be commercially viable.

In many states, the progress of infrastructure reforms especially in the field of irrigation is not adequate. Definitely private investment in the field of development of irrigation facilities will help to utilize available water resources in an economic and efficient manner. This will go a long way in improving the economic conditions of the people of rural areas of the States.

One of the most important items in the list of hurdles to the country's economic growth is poor infrastructural facilities. This is especially true of the transport sector. If ports are to be de-congested, proper roads constructed and the large but rickety rail network brought on track, India must invest significantly and without undue delay. But with the fiscal deficit hovering at around 10% of GDP and committed expenditures difficult to cut, there is need to find alternative sources of fund. M.S. Ahluwalia, the Deputy Chairman of Planning Commission some time back suggested the idea of drawing the funds ($ 5 billion a year) from the foreign exchange reserves of the country. Precisely, Union

Finance Minister P.Chidambaram's Budget for 2005–06, proposes a special purpose vehicle (SPV) to implement the infrastructure projects that are financially viable but encounter problems in mobilizing resources. The FM wants to draw on the foreign exchange reserves, especially for project imports. Also, there is need for releasing certain norms governing external commercial borrowings (ECBs) to enable Indian Companies borrow abroad at lower cost for making investment in the financially viable infrastructure projects.

Transport is emerged as the principal loss makers of the States along with power. As suggested by Planning Commission Study Group, the Road Transport Corporations need to improve bus-staff ratio, occupancy ratio, fleet management and estate management practices. The innovative involvement of the private sector in the fleet could also improve their earnings.

5. Fiscal Reforms

Government of India's efforts to improve and strengthen the finances of the States is a healthy development but the most important aspect is that the states themselves have to participate in the process of fiscal consolidation. The economic reforms of the States should aim at reducing unproductive public expenditures, improving the economic performance of PSUs and making infrastructural facilities commercially viable.

Concluding Remarks

The economic reforms introduced in the country in the mid–1991 have created new dynamism and their progress in the last 14 years has been reasonably good. The ER policy measures are percolated gradually, from centre where they were initiated to the States in a considerable way. In the past several years, various political parties belonging to different ideology have come to power in the States and the Centre. They have taken up and continue to sustain bold economic reform measures embracing a wide range of activities. The ERs implemented so far have helped India to attain on an average more than five per cent growth. This can be considered as a legitimate achievement of the economic reforms. Still there is long way to go. Government of

India and the States need to fasten reforms at the State level to check prevalent rampant corruption, to improve the efficiency in administration and quality in development works.

The public expenditure policy should be reoriented in such a way as to reduce unproductive expenditures and increase public spending in high priority areas such as development of irrigation facilities and other social and economic infrastructural facilities. The ER measures should also aim at inducing private investment in eco-friendly economic activities such as small wind and hydropower generation, biomass, municipal solid waste management and production of bio-manure and sugar factory cogeneration projects, development of parks, Tourism centres, etc., when all these measures are undertaken in earnest, it is likely to attain and sustain targeted eight percent of economic growth.

References

Ahluwalia, Montek S. (2003) "The Economic Performance of the States in the Post Reforms Period" in Ed. Kapila, Uma., Indian Economy Since Independence (New Delhi, Academic Foundation).

Datt, Ruddar (2000) "Second Generation Reforms : Need for Changing Growth Strategy", IEA 83rd Conference Volume.

Editorial (2005) "Funding Infrastructure" The Hindu Business Line Vol.12, No.68, March 10.

George, K.K. (2002) "Major Issues in State Level Fiscal Reforms" IEA 85th Conference Volume.

Godbole, Madhav (2002) "Power Sector Reforms : If Wishes were Horses" EPW Vol. XXXVII, No.7, Feb. 16.

Government of Karnataka (2002) "Karnataka – Tomorrow's Destination Today, Advertiser's Feature" The Hindu, Jan 10.

Government of Karnataka (2005) "Economic Survey 2004–05" (Bangalore : Planning and Statistics Department).

Gurumurthy, S. (2002) "Twelfth Finance Commission and States' Debt Burden" EPW Vol. XXXVII, No.40, October 5.

Heggade, Odeyar D. and Bharathi M.R. (2000) "Second Generation Economic Reforms in India : Issues and Directions", IEA 83rd Conference Volume

Jayanth, V. (2005) "States and Their Finances" The Hindu March 7, Vol. 128, No.55.

Kurien, N.J. (2005) Report of the Study Group on State Finances, Planning Commission, Press Report, The Hindu, April 16.

Naik, S.D. (2004) "Power Sector Reforms May Derail" The Hindu Business Line Vol. 11, No.222, Aug. 10.

Palande, P.S. (2000) "Coping with Liberalisation - The Industry's Response to New Competition" (New Delhi : Response Books).

Prasad, K.N. (2003) "Indian Economy – Before and Since the Reforms" Vol. IV (New Delhi, Atlantic Publishers and Distributors).

Rangarajan, C. (2004) "Restructuring Public Finances for Equitable Growth – Issues Before the Twelfth Finance Commission". EPW, Vol. XXXIX, No. 26, June 26.

Rao, S L. (2003) "Electricity Bill, 2001, Many Shortcoming, But a Step Forward" EPW, Vol. XXXVIII, No.5, Feb. 1–7.

CHAPTER 10

The Third Sector Participation in Social Forestry—A felt Need in India

Rationale and Theoretical Background

Natural resources of earth ship are finite, if we misuse them continuously, they will eventually exhaust. Long back Alfred Marshall, David Ricardo, Thomas Robert Malthus have warned their countrymen about the limited supply of natural resources. In our times, Joseph Cornellens Kumarappa, Club of Rome under the Stewardship of Dennis Meadows and Brundtland Commission, Lester R. Brown and others have made marvellars studies about the precious characteristic features of natural resources.

J.C. Kumarappa's concept of Economy of Permanence

According to JCK, work in nature consists in the effort putforth by the various factors - insentient and sentient – which cooperate to complete the cycle of life. If this cycle is broken, at any time, consciously or unconsciously, violence results as a consequence of such a break. When violence intervenes, growth or progress is stopped, ending finally in destruction and waste. Nature is unforgiving and merciless. Therefore, self-interest and self-preservation demand complete non-violence, cooperation and submission to the ways of nature if we are to maintain permanency by non-interference with and by not short-circuiting the cycle of life. Six decades back, Kumarappa advocated what we call today Sustainable Development long before the term entered the lexicon.

The Club of Rome Model

In 1972, the Club of Rome Published Report "The Limits to Growth". Its main conclusion was that, if the present growth trends in population, food production, industrialization, pollution and resource depletion continue, the limits to economic growth on a global basis will be reached within the next 100 years. This conclusion was based on a study directed by Dennis Meadows and conducted at the MIT since the study was initiated by the Club of Rome, an in formal international association of individuals, it is generally referred to as the Club of Rome Study or Model. The study finds only two possibilities: either we impose limits to growth or nature will. The latter leads to collapse. Consequently the group claims that the only reasonable alternative is the former and, given the nature of exponential growth, we must undertake policies designed to limit growth soon.

Plan B Model of Lester Brown

Lester R. Brown, the founder President of the Earth Policy Institute, Washington is a droughty green warrior of impeccable credentials. According to him, Planet Earth is in peril as evidenced by burgeoning under-nourished populations, the HIV / AIDS menace, water stress, falling land productivity and adverse climate change induced by green house gas build-up in the atmosphere. Brown shares the grim view of many scientists that the biggest threat to mankind's survival may arise out of global warming. Of the Green house gases, the most prominent one namely carbon dioxide is emitted by the burning of fossil fuels. Plan B's messages make one reminiscent the prognosis made by the Brundtland Commission (1987) almost two decades back. The call for sustainable development is being heard but sadly not still acted upon vigorously.

The Brundtland Commission (1987) puts the notion of Sustainable Development on the international agenda and emphasizes the need for merging economics and environment in decision making. According to it, the need for merger emanates from the existence of and pervasive nature of environmental externalities, institutional myopia and sectoral self-interest

Social Forestry in India

India's forest cover has been put at 19.52% of land area. India still far short of the ideal 33.33% that ecologists hold the country should try to achieve and maintain. At least five to 10 million hectares of degraded land need to be brought under forests annually to maintain. At least five to 10 million hectares of degraded land need to be brought under forests annually to maintain the ecological balance in the country. Also forestation helps in a big way for the removal poverty, unemployment and pollution problems of the country.

Government of India launched Vana Mahotasava (forests celebrations), Save Himalaya Movement, Make India Green campaign and other forestry programmes for increasing forestry coverage in the country (1950). The social forestry (SF) programme was first started in 1976. The basic idea of this programme is to involve the non-government organizations and people in raising their own forests on their own lands and surroundings for their benefit and benefit of the country as a whole.

Components of Social Forestry

There are threes components of SF viz., Agro-forestry, Rural forestry and Urban forestry. The AF aims at inculcating tree culture practices among farmers. Farmers are encouraged to plant fruit yielding frees. Farmers generally produce food grains but do not cater to fuel. This leads to overished use of cattle dung as fuel for cooking and heating in the rural areas. Cattle-dung along with litter and green leaves makes an organic manure which serves as life-blood to the soil. Its scarcity seriously affects soil fertility. The AF aims at averting this problem and converting it into a positive annual gain by the creation of eco-friendly / human friendly green coverage in the farms. The variety of plants and trees planted in the farms will help the farmers to get fruits, vegetables, greens, fire wood, fodder, timber and other economic benefits like increase in the fertility of soil and water deposits in the farms.

The RF calls for forestation programmes on community and village lands, degraded forests, roads, railways and canal sides for the benefit of rural people. The ownership system is community based. The basic objective of RF is to lift farmers out of their conditions of economics backwardness and help them attain self-sufficiency through planting of trees.

The UF is a best remedy for keeping towns and cities beautiful, clean and making them livable and lovable. The solid and liquid wastes of the towns and cities can be converted into organic manures which help the local governments to generate additional sources of income. The city waste water after extracting its solid manure, can be utilized for forestation programme in and around Towns / Cities which helps to control air pollution, water pollution and also the growth of slum areas. The UF may also be known as recreational forestry. The RCF has two fold objectives – to bring trees on the door step of the urban people and to improve the aesthetics of local surroundings. Tree species of diversity which flower, yield fruits, income at different seasons and become timber of high value are planted in different places of towns and cities.

Involvement of Third Sector in S.F.

Voluntary Organisations (VOs) around the world are playing a very important role in creating public opinion in favour of development of forest resources. VOs can make efforts to plant trees in and around Government, Private Offices, other institutional complexes, sports bodies, and cultural centres. With concerted efforts the VOs could be involved in mobilizing the masses for taking up forestation of the available wasteland in the villages, towns and cities with a missionary zeal. VOs have an advantages of working at the grass roots lends for the overall community development.

Methodology

This study is wholly based on secondary data. However, some field study is made on the functioning of VOs involved in S.F. in Mysore city. In this context special mention may be made of World Environmental Services Organisation (WESO) of Mysore which was set up in 1998. It is a non-political, secular multi-lingual and a non-regional service organization. The WESO aims at cleaning Mysore and planting trees of diverse variety under SF programme with the help of State Government and other service organizations. It organizes quiz programmes, special lectures, seminars on tree plantation. It has planted thousands of trees in different parts of Mysore. For the purpose of this paper, 50 members of this organization are contacted. Environmentalists, Engineers, Scientists, Lawyers, Doctors, Students, Teachers, Factory Personnel, Retired Persons are actively involved as its members.

Findings of the Study

The SF has its own characteristic features which differentiate it from conventional forestry. There are various difficulties for the Government of deal with SF programme, traditions, structures, attitudes, needs and aspirations of Rural people and Urban people differ widely from one area to another. So there is a need to involve VOs and encourage the people to participate in SF programme, that means VOs can act as bridges between the Government and the aspirations of the people.

But the VOs have their strengths and weaknesses. Their activities are diverse. The real strength of VOs is their grass root contact. One of the weakness of the VOs is that there is no worth-while forum, local, regional and much less national for exchange of experience and unified action for the delivery of inputs adversely affect for the delivery of inputs adversely affect the activities of these organizations.

Suggestions

Government should support the VOs that have ability to work with the economically weaker sections of the society. The effort should be to build up a god local resource base and a strong infrastructure that support other organizations in the area. VOs need helping in one or more of the areas enumerated below.

1. An in–depth study of SF and of the need of the people's active participation in the programme should be taken up.
2. People should be made known about the benefits of SF in the context of global warming, and their economic well-being by the VOs, extension staff, and other institutions through different extension, methods, literature, posters, charts, photographs, field trips and other males.

3. Seeds banks should be established for making available seeds to nursery growers.
4. The schools/collages/universities, in assistance with State and Union Governments, should organize training, seminars/conferences/workshops from time to time to exchange ideas among field workers, village people government functionaries, public leaders etc., on various aspects of SF.
5. The study of environment in the curriculum educational institutions should be made compulsory text books should be prescribed for creating awareness among students on the harmful effects of forestation and the immediate needs of SF.
6. Proper selection of plant species and sites of plantation should be followed in consultation with the experts and local persons both according to the need and suitability of the areas concerned.
7. Also, there should be proper interaction among staff of the forest department, VOs, local governments, peoples representatives and local people involved in the execution of the SF programmes.

Conclusion Remarks

There are various facilities extended by Government for the implementation of S.F programme. The SF programme should be self propelling, self sustaining and largely a self–reliant movement of the people. Multiple use of land and use of multipurpose, indigenous trees with proven advantages for enhancing fertility of soil, apart from giving various economic benefits to the people should govern the SF programme. The active role of Government Staff and VOs is of paramount importance for ideal implementation of SF programme.

References

1. Marie Bystrom (2004), "Integration of biodiversity aspects in development co-operation- a case study" Environment Policy Division.www.sida.se/publications.

2. Nilsson. et al (2000), "Trees in the Environment", Oxford University Press, Newark.
3. "Social Forestry in India". www.wikipedia.com
4. Nagothu Udaya Sekhar and Ivar Jorgensen(2003), "Social Forestry in South Asia: Myths and Realities", Noragric Working Paper No.30
5. Mcpherson, E.G. (1998), "Structure and Sustainability of Sacramento's urban forest", Journal of Arboriculture 24(4):174-190.
6. Jacob E. John and Melvin Louis (2008), "Social Forestry with fruit trees: A role for herbivores and village children", Current Science.
7. Sathaye J.A. and et.al (2001), "Carbonmitigation potential and costs of forestry options in Brazil, China, India, Indonesia, Maxico, the Philippines and Tanzania", Kluwer Academic Publishers, 6,185.
8. Involvement of village community and VAs in generation of degraded forests (1990).http: //iifm.ac.in/databank.

CHAPTER 11

Social Forestry and Role in Rural Development

Abstract

The life of a segment of the population is faced with many difficulties; especially in the rural areas. Unemployment and lack of basic need like food, fresh drinking water, shelters, cloths and education still there in rural side. To bring our country out of underemployment and improve the socio-economic, socio-cultural and spiritual life of rural people's social forestry is an effective tool in India. This paper summarizes the studies of effects of social forestry on the socio -economic, socio-cultural development of rural peoples in India. Social forestation based rural development aspects explained the agricultural and environmental importance of forestation in rural side in India. The socio – economic and socio-cultural conditions of rural peoples in India directly or indirectly depend on the natural resources and their availability around their habitation. Social forestation in the rural side promoting directly or indirectly ecological and economical developments in rural peoples through involving them in social forestation and basic skills along with cultural and moral education. Social forestation activities in the rural areas, the helps to local people participation in public meeting espically rural women's participation in public meeting is a considerable fact and it helps to gain basic knowledge about importance of forest and its conservation in rural areas.

Introduction

The term 'social forestry' was first used in 1976 by the National Commission on Agriculture, Government of India, to describe forestry on village not forest reserve land. It was then that India embarked upon a social forestry project with the aim of taking the pressure off the forests and making use of all unused and fallow land. Government forest areas that are close to human settlement and have been degraded over the years due to human activities needed to be afforested. Trees were to be planted in and around agricultural fields. Plantation of trees along railway lines and roadsides and river and canal banks were carried out. They were planted in village common land, Government wasteland and Panchayat land. Social forestry also aims at raising plantations by the common man so as to meet the growing demand for timber, fuel wood, fodder, etc, thereby reducing the pressure on the traditional forest area. This concept of village forests to meet the needs of the rural people is not new. It has existed through the centuries all over the country but it was now given a new character. With the introduction of this scheme the government formally recognized the local communities' rights to forest resources, and is now encouraging rural participation in the management of natural resources. Through the social forestry scheme, the government has involved community participation, as part of a drive towards afforestation, and rehabilitating the degraded forest and common lands. Social forestry is, in effect, an integral part of the Gandhian philosophy of economic growth and community development. Imagine an economy in which the present idle land and water resources, owned by individuals or communities, are harnessed for better purposes by putting to work unemployed people. The social benefits thus generated and the additional resources so created may serve as stepping stones toward self-sufficiency.

Its main components are- farm forestry, community forestry, extension forestry and agro-forestry. Broadly speaking, their objectives are almost identical, the differences being too subtle, but worth examining.

Farm forestry

At present in all most all the countries where social forestry programmes have been taken up, both commercial and noncommercial farm forestry is being promoted to one farm or the other. Individual farmers are being encouraged to plant trees on their own farmland to meet the domestic needs of the family.

In many areas this tradition of growing trees on the farmland already exists. Non-commercial farm forestry is the main thrust of most of the social forestry projects in the country today. It is not always necessary that the grows trees for fuel wood, but very often they are interested in growing trees without any economic motive. They may want it to provide shade for the agricultural crops; as wind shelters; soil conservation or t use wasteland.

Community forestry

Another scheme taken up under the social forestry programme, it is the raising of trees on community land and not on private land as in farm forestry. All these programmes aim to provide for the entire community and not for any individual. The government has the responsibility of providing seedlings, fertilizer but the community has to take responsibility of protecting the trees. Some communities manage the plantation sensibly and in a sustainable manner so that the village continues to benefit. Some others took advantage and sold the timber for a short-term individual profit. Common land being everyone's land is very easy to exploit. Over the last 20 years, large-scale planting of Eucalyptus, as a fast growing exotic, has occurred in India, making it a part of the drive to reforest the subcontinent and create an adequate supply of timber for rural communities under the augur of "social forestry"

Extension forestry

Planting of trees on the sides of roads, canals and railways, along with planting on wastelands is known as 'extension' forestry, increasing the boundaries of forestry. Under this project there has been creation of wood lots in the village common lands, government wastelands and panchayat lands. Schemes for afforesting degraded government forests that are close villages are being carried out all over the country.

Agro-forestry

In agro-forestry silvicultural practices are combined with agricultural crops like leguminous crop, along with orchard farming and livestock ranching on the same piece of land. In a lay man language agro-forestry could be understood as growing of forest tree along with agriculture crop on the same piece of land. In a more scientific way agro-forestry may be defined as a sustainable land use system that maintains or increases the total yield by combing food crop together with forest tree and live stock ranching on the same unit of land using management practices that takes care of the social and culture characteristic of the local people and the economic and ecological condition of the local area.

The objectives of social forestry

Social forestry schemes that have been started all over the country have made a considerable difference in overall forest cover in a short time. Social forestations outside the conventional forest area have the benefit of rural and urban communities. The main objectives of the social forestry are as follows:

1. Improve the environment for protecting agriculture from adverse climatic factors,
2. Increase the supply of fuel wood for domestic use, small timber for rural housing, fodder for livestock, and forest produce for local industries.
3. Increase the natural beauty of the landscape; create recreational forests for the benefit of rural and urban population,
4. Provide jobs for unskilled workers and
5. Reclaim wastelands.
6. Finally, the main object social forestry is to increases the living standards and of the rural and urban peoples.

Role of social forestry in rural development

I. Economic aspects

Social forestry provides contribution to improve economic conditions of the rural population by following aspects:

1. Less investment capital and more profits.
2. Unused and wasteland used for social forestation

3. They provide required fuel woods and small timbers houses and households
4. They provide jobs for the uneducated rural peoples
5. They provide by-products like fruits, seeds and medicine leafs
6. Tourism and recreationai activities improve economic condition of the rural peoples
7. Bio-diesel production in India is totally depend on the social forest products
8. They provide the aid of tree resources and support to the cottage industries in rural areas.

2. Agriculture aspect

Social forestry provides contribution to improve agricultural conditions of the rural population by following aspects:

a) The achievement of soil stability, water conservation and freedom from wind erosion damage.
b) They provide required food for poultry industry.
c) They also provide raw materials for bio-fertilizer/ composting
d) Trees planted on farm boundaries serve as protection fences and shelterbelts
e) They provide required equipments for agriculture purposes
f) They provide highly effective forests products which are used as an insecticides and pesticides.

3. Environmental aspects

Social forestry provides contribution to improve ecological conditions of the rural population by following aspects:

a) Decrease air pollution and CO_2 content in atmosphere
b) Avoid soil erosion and loss of fertility
c) Avoid noise pollution
d) Increase the atmospheric moisture
e) Control floods
f) Increase ground water table by infiltration of water through soil
g) Increases the bio-diversity
h) Decreases the atmospheric temperature

i) They works as effective wind breakers

5. Cultural aspects

Social forestry provides contribution to improve cultural activities of the rural population by following aspects:

a) Participation of rural women and young peoples in conservation forest and it importance
b) Environmental education and awareness in rural peoples
c) Plantation skills developments in uneducated rural peoples
d) Skills for usage of waste lands and uncultivated lands
e) Public participation skills, improve initiative, self-help and self reliance in rural people

All the above mentioned factors help to the rural development. The social forestation improves the socio-economic and socio-cultural conditions of rural peoples directly or indirectly.

Conclusion

There are many ways to sustainable development of rural areas and social forestry is one of the effective and important methods for the rural development in India. Social forestry is directly or indirectly improves the soci-economic and socio-cultural conditions of the rural peoples. Social forestation in rural areas also provides basic needs and requirements for their daily life and agricultural activities. The multiple benefits from farm forestry to the rural economy are intended to accrue without impairing the normal field productivity. It encompasses forestry activities on community and village lands, degraded forests, road and railway sides and canal banks for the benefit of rural people. It also includes restoration of derelict areas such as those bearing scars of quarrying, mining road construction, brick manufacture, lime burning and the like. At the same time, there are about 220 million people, mainly in the rural areas, who are living below the poverty line because they are either unemployed or underemployed. Given appropriate incentives and training, these idle people can be productively employed to afforest substantial rural land hither to untapped. Social forestry all improves the biodiversity and environment quality.

References

1. Divya M.P. and et al (2008), "Social Forestry and Agro forestry", Sathish Serial Publishing House, New Delhi, P.316.
2. Marie Bystrom (2004), "Integration of biodiversity aspects in development co-operation- a case study" Environment Policy Division.www.sida.se/publications.
3. Nilsson. et al (2000), "Trees in the Environment", Oxford University Press, Newark.
4. "Social Forestry in India". www.wikipedia.com
5. Mcpherson, E.G. (1998), "Structure and Sustainability of Sacramento's urban forest", Journal of Arboriculture 24(4):174-190.
6. Jacob E. John and Melvin Louis (2008), "Social Forestry with fruit trees: A role for herbivores and village children", Current Science.
7. Sathaye J.A. and et.al (2001), "Carbonmitigation potential and costs of forestry options in Brazil, China, India, Indonesia, Maxico, the Philippines and Tanzania", Kluwer Academic Publishers, 6,185.
8. Involvement of village community and VAs in generation of degraded forests (1990).http: //iifm.ac.in/databank.
9. Nagothu Udaya Sekhar and Ivar Jorgensen(2003), "Social Forestry in South Asia: Myths and Realities", Noragric Working Paper No.30

CHAPTER 12

Agriculature Marketing in Karnataka —An Analysis of Problems and Improvement Programmes

Kohls and Douney defines agricultural marketing as the performance of all business activities involved in the movement of goods and services from the point of initial agricultural production until they are in the hands of the ultimate buyers. Thus, agriculture marketing includes all marketing activities involved in transforming, storing and the movement of agricultural produces from the production points starting from the stage of harvest till they reach the ultimate consumers. Marketing of the produces grown in agriculture is equally important as producing them. Marketing of the agro produces at remunerative prices stimulates production and consumption and overall economic development. A very important part in the process of agricultural development is the creation of proper marketing facilities and in the absence of proper marketing facilities the basic economic functions of agricultural production, distribution and consumption are going to be very much affected. Well developed marketing facilities and ideal organization of marketing are very important to get full benefit of agricultural production. The agricultural sector of India has seen an increase in market surplus over a period of 50 years after independence of the country. The increased surplus calls for a rapid improvement in the marketing infrastructure.

The farmers who grow the agricultural produces are finding it difficult to get suitable prices for their output. It is a painful thing to say that in a way, they have been continuously robbing. The UNCTAD report not only substantiates it but also goes much beyond the computation done by the Union Agriculture Ministry. The prices which farmers are getting for their output are the same at which they were selling their produces 20 years ago. A recent study of the Union Agriculture Ministry had shown that the incomes from the agriculture have fallen in the past five years.

Paddy growers of West Bengal (2002–2003) had earned 28 percent less than what they earned in 1996-97. In Uttar Pradesh, incomes of sugarcane growers have decreased by 32 percent and Maharashtra by 40 percent during the same period. But while the advanced countries made up for the loss of incomes in agriculture by providing direct payments first linked to production and now linked to the farm area, agriculturists in India continued to suffer silently. In order to help the farmers to get remunerative prices for their produces proper agricultural marketing system is of great importance.

Now, it is increasingly recognised that the agricultural marketing system is so important in economic development not only for physically distributing increased production but also for distributing the benefits of economic growth. With the introduction of the economic reform policy measures and emergence of WTO conditionalities many changes have taken place including macroeconomic stabilization and structural reforms designed to integrate the domestic economy to world economy. These changes naturally exerted their own impact on agricultural marketing. The most significant development that is noticed is that these developments revolved a round marketing, necessitating the need for formulating an appropriate marketing policy to get the benefits of international trade under the WTO policy regime.

Regulated Marketing in India - An Inter-State Comparison

In the regulated marketing system of India, marketing of the agricultural produce will be made through a kind of government intervention

Table 1: State / UT-wise Distribution of Regulated Markets in India (As on March 2004)

S. no	State	*Regulated Markets*		
		Main Market	*Sub Market*	*Total*
1.	Andhra Pradesh	299	590	889 (11.98)
2.	Arunachala Pradesh	—	—	—
3.	Assam	21	19	40 (0.54)

4.	Bihar	95	415	510 (6.88)
5.	Jharkhand	27	276	303 (4.08)
6.	Goa	01	07	08 (0.11)
7.	Gujarat	181	222	403 (3.83)
8.	Haryana	106	178	284 (3.83)
9.	Himachal pradesh	08	27	35 (0.47)
10.	Jammu and Kashmir APMR Act is not implemented in the State			
11.	Karnataka	145	351	496 (6.69)
12.	Kerala	APMR Act is not yet enacted		
13.	Madhya Pradesh	233	252	485 (6.54)
14.	Chhatisgarh	73	104	177 (2.39)
15.	Maharashtra	276	595	871 (11.74)
16.	Manipur	APMR Act is not yet enacted		
17.	Meghahaya	—	—	—
18.	Mizzoram	—	—	—
19.	Nagaland	—	—	—
20.	Orissa	45	380	425 (5.73)
21.	Punjab	145	292	437 (5.89)
22.	Rajastan	124	289	413 (5.57)
23.	Sikkim	—	—	—
24.	Tamil Nadu	273	14	287 (3.88)
25.	Tripura	21	—	21 (0.28)
26.	Uttar Pradesh	245	340	585 (7.89)
27.	Uttaranchal	25	32	57 (0.77)
28.	West Bengal	45	617	662 (8.92)
29.	Andaman and Nicobar Islands	APMR Act is not yet enacted		
30.	Chandigarh	01	01	01 (0.01)
31.	Dadar and Nagar haveli	APMR Act is not yet enacted		
32.	Daman & Diu	—	—	—
33.	Delhi	09	12	21 (0.28)
34.	Lakshdweep	APMR Act is not yet enacted		
35.	Pondicherry	04	03	07 (0.09)
		2402 (100.00)	5016(100.00)	7418 (100.00)

and that is in the form of market regulation. The principal objectives of market regulation policy of Government of India are to improve the marketing system by regulating malpractices in the marketing of the agricultural outputs, decreasing marketing costs and providing reasonable marketing facilities to farmers. The rationale behind regulated marketing system is to make available benefits to the farmers, which would encourage them to specialize in their agricultural production. It also induces the farmers for the commercialization of agriculture which is very essential for economic development. Also, regulated marketing system helps to increase marketing efficiency, check the superfluous market intermediaries and further integration in the marketing system.

In India, 23 states have established regulated markets. As at March 2004, there were 7418 regulated markets in the country. Andhra Pradesh (11.98%) has the largest number of markets, the next largest number are in Maharashtra (11.74%) followed by West Bengal (8.92%), Uttara Pradesh (7.89%), Bihar (6.88%), Karnataka (6.69%), Madhya Pradesh (6.54%), Punjab (5.89%), Orissa (5.73%), Rajastan (5.57%), Gujrath (5.43%), Jharkand (4.08%), Tamil Nadu (3.88%), Haryana (3.83%) and Chhatisghar (2.39%). While it is below one percent in Uttaranchal, Assam, Himachal Pradesh, Goa, Tripura, Chandigarh, Delhi and Pondicherry States / Union Territories; Jammu and Kashmir, Kerala, Manipur, Andaman and Nicobar, Dhadar and Nagar Haveli and Lakshadweep have not implemented the APMC Act (as at March 2004).

Agricultural Marketing Programmes in Karnataka

In Karnataka, the Agricultural Produce Marketing (Regulation) Act was enacted in 1966 with a view to providing a uniform legislation pertaining to better regulation of buying and selling of agricultural produce and the establishment of markets for agricultural produce in different parts of the state.Under section 100 of 1966 Act, the Karnataka State Agricultural Marketing Board was set up in September 1972. The Board Acts as a liaison institution between the agricultural marketing committees and the State Government for the development of agricultural marketing activities in the state. The important functions of the Board are grading and standarisation of agricultural produce, general improvement of the regulation of agricultural marketing, providing loans to needy agricultural marketing committees, publicity, agricultural marketing, improvement of transport facilities, advising the State Government on the matters related to agricultural marketing, and implementing the welfare schemes for farmers, weighmen, hamals and care persons etc. The Board has set up two training centers through which officers of the marketing department, the Board, and APMCs are given training in the matters of agricultural development. Also, farmers, market committee members, members of Panchayat raj institutions are given training in the matters of agricultural marketing.

Table 2: Value of Transactions of Agricultural Produce in Karnataka

Year	*Transaction (Rs. in Crores)*
2000 – 2001	7,512.00
2001 – 2002	7,902.00
2002 – 2003	8,128.00
2003 – 2004	8,437.00
2004 – 2005 (Upto Dec. 2004)	7,200.00

Source: Government of Karnataka, Dept. of Cooperation, 100 Years of Cooperative Movement - 1905 - 2005.

The beginning of the agricultural marketing system was made, with the establishment of the agricultural produce market at Bailahongal in 1936. Another agricultural produce market was set up in Tiptur in 1948. As at March 2004, there were 144 main APMCs and 343 sub-APMCs in the State. To administer the agricultural produce regulated markets, there is a separate Directorate by name Directorate of Agricultural Marketing. It administers regulation of sale and purchase of agriculture produce brought by agriculturists to the market yards providing a forum to ensure competitive prices, right weighment, payment and creating an exploitation–free ecology by checking illegal activities in the marketing of the products of agriculturists.

Agriculture Market Development Programmes in Karnataka

Agriculture marketing development programmes are undertaken under two schemes namely: State Sector and Central Sector Schemes.

State Sector Schemes

With a view to developing agricultural markets all over the state and to supplement the efforts of APMCs in providing infrastructure facilities in the market yards and for better utilization of funds, State Government has developed two schemes namely market price scheme and minimum floor price scheme.

Under market infrastructure scheme, infrastructure facilities like shop-cum-godowns, auction platforms, rest houses for farmers, internal roads, compounds, drinking water, canteen, post office, banks, street lights, facilities for cattle trading are being made available by APMCs. The minimum floor price scheme was introduced in Nov. 1999, this scheme is implemented for providing price stability and to protect the interests of farmers against distress sale of agro produces by assuring a floor price.

Central Sector Scheme

There are mainly two Central Government Schemes and they are macro management of agriculture and pledge loan scheme. Under the macro management scheme, the Central Government releases grants to supplement / complement the state efforts in the field of agricultural marketing towards the development of infrastructure facilities. Under the pledge loan scheme, farmers are protected from the fall in the price of agricultural commodities. Under this scheme, agriculturalists can pledge their produce in the market committee godowns or in State / Central warehouse godowns and avail of short term loan to the maximum of Rs.50,000/- for a period of three months.

Development of Rural Shandies

Rural shandies are established under Rural Infrastructure Development Fund Scheme (RIDF). As at December 2004, under this scheme, 29 rural markets have been developed at a cost of Rs.445 lakhs. Development of 13 rural markets have been taken up at a cost of Rs.242.90 lakhs. For the development of these rural markets, the NABARD has sanctioned a loan amount of Rs.218.60 lakhs (works completed). Development of rural markets are taken up at a cost of Rs.200.94 lakhs under the RIDF VII scheme. For the development of Rural markets, NABARD has sanctioned Rs.180.86 lakhs as loan. The cabinet sub-committee has sanctioned the scheme for the development of 222 Rural markets at a cost of Rs.2500/- lakhs under the RIDF-X scheme. NABARD has sanctioned an amount of Rs.2105.56 lakhs for the development of 193 rural markets at a cost of Rs.2216.13 lakhs, which includes Government contribution of Rs.110.58 lakhs. The works of 193 rural markets amounting to Rs.2342.17 lakhs for which administrative approval and technical sanction have been given out of which 10 works have been completed and the remaining works are in progress.

Farmers Shandies

With view to helping the farmers to become economically viable, the State Government has decided to organize farmers shandies in all the taluks of the state step by step. As a first step, farmers shandies are functioning at Hubli and Yelahanka in Bangalore. The construction works of farmers shandies at Bidar, Ranebennur, Haveri, Maddur and Bijapur, are completed. Farmers shandies are also coming up at Bagalkot and Basavana Bagewadi. Farmers shandies provide an ideal place for direct interface between farmers and buyers of the agro produces. Farmers shandies help the farmers to get remunerative prices for their produces as middlemen's interference is not there. Consumers get fresh produces at reasonable prices. The farmers get the full share of what the consumers pay.

Market Information Programmes

Krishimarata vahini scheme is introduced to provide uptodate market information to the farmers. The department of agricultural marketing has launched Krishi Marata Vahini web-site for this purpose. This website is connected to AGMARK Net Website of the Directorate of Marketing and Inspection, Government of India. In Karnataka, 143 APMC's have been provided with computers fitted with internet facility for the purpose. The major APMCs enter the data on a day-to-day basis on the centralized server. The APMCs collect data and update the data with reference to arrivals, minimum, maximum, model prices of commodities traded on line.

Computerization of Commodity Tender System

Under the Central Sector Scheme an amount of Rs.15 lakhs each is extended to Mysore and Bellary APMCs for computerizing the

Commodity Tender System. National Informatics Centre has been entrusted with the work of implementing the project on a turnkey basis.

Construction of Onion Godowns in Farmers' Fields

The Karnataka State Agricultural Marketing Board in collaboration with the National Horticulture Research Foundation (Nasik) has formulated a scheme of constructing onion godowns of 10, 20 and 50 MTs in the farmers fields.

Agricultural Marketing Reform Measures of Karnataka

On the advice of Government of India, Karnataka has introduced various agricultural marketing reform measures. Now the whole state has been treated as a single market. The levy of market fee is at a single point in the state from October 2001. Also, 113 agricultural commodities have been uniformly notified in all the 144 APMCs to facilitate hassle free regulation. Market fee exemption has been given (March 2003) to the trade in Gherkin which is grown under contract farming and totally exported. Cashew kernel has been de-regulated as it has large export potential. The exemption of market fee helps to augment exports of this commodity. With a view to further simplifying the levy of market fee, the State Government has enacted legislation that provides for the exemption of market fee on processed agricultural commodities. In order to give the cooperatives an important role in the marketing system, a provision has been made to either totally exempt or fix concessional rates of market fee on their transactions. Also cooperative institutions have been given the opportunity of doing wholesale trade any where in the market area.

Framing of Allotment Rules

The allotment rules have been formulated for allotment of sites, shop-cum-godowns, sundry shops, weigh bridges, canteens etc. on leave - and license and lease-cum-sale basis. With the enactment of these rules, a uniform system of allotment has been enforced. Also, it ensures transparency and a system of equitable allotment of the properties of the market committees to the market functionaries and other stake-holders.

Problems of Agricultural Marketing and Suggestions for improvement

Like irrigation and credit facilities, marketing facilities are also very important. They immensely help to induce the growth of agriculture. But the position of marketing of the agricultural produces is highly miserable, in this connection farmers have to face so many hardships. Even now large number of farmers are poor, they are under the debt obligations. Their waiting capacity for getting good prices is very less. Hence, they are compelled to dispose of their produce at distress rates to the intermediaries. Also, most of the village farmers do not have safe storing facilities. Farmers also have to incur heavy transport expenditure. In between bringing and selling their produces in the market farmers cannot get hygienic food and needed rest. Most of the farmers are ignorant of ruling market prices and weighing and measuring systems. In the midst of large number of intermediacies farmers are not able to get remunerative prices for their produces. In order to provide remunerative prices to the farmers, to control unhealthy market practices, to reduce exorbitant marketing charges and to provide basic facilities for marketing, regulated markets have been established.

Karnataka has vast institutional network for agricultural marketing. There are 487 main and sub-agricultural markets in the State. Of this, 220 are established in 15 districts of South Karnataka (45.17%) and 267 (57.83%) are located in 12 districts of north Karnataka. But, when we look at the number of markets and their turnover it comes to our notice that some districts fall shortage of the marketing centres. When we compare to the state average (5.99%) of markets and their turnover, districts like Raichur, Koppal, Haveri, Mysore, Kodagu, Dakshina Kannada, Shimoga, Davanagere and Bangalore (Urban) do not have adequate number of markets for providing marketing benefits to the farmers. Even now there are various taluks which do not have agricultural markets. Secondly, in various taluks, market facilities are not developed for items such as potato, chillies, maize, mango and other agricultural and horticultural produces. Thirdly, marketing activities are enlarging, hence, these is need for proper maintenance of marketing centers by providing good accommodation facility, hygienic food, cleanliness, proper watch and ward etc. Fourthly, there is need for maintaining proper transparency in the matters of market prices, quantity of goods arriving to the markets and their disposal. Farmers are needed to keep informed about the nature of prices for different produces, the variety of goods which had come to the markets in the previous weeks and other useful aspects of marketing. This is possible with the adaptation of information technology in the market yards.

In order to increase exports of agricultural produces suitable marketing facilities have to be created in the rural areas also. Most of the farmers are ignorant of the international marketing conditions, hence suitable information and training about exports and export markets are to be imparted among the farmers, so that they can grow good quality produces and prepare well to export them to international markets. Government of Karnataka has fixed a target of increasing exports to the extent of 20% and to facilitate to achieve this target suitable stocking, processing and warehousing facilities have to be created in the districts and taluks head quarters. To promote warehousing facilities in the villages and semi-urban areas, the cooperation of the panchayatraj institutions and rural co-operative societies are to be sought.

Table 3: Agricultural Markets in Karnataka

District	*Main Markets*	*Sub Markets*	*Total Markets*	*Turnover (Rs. Crores)*	*No. of Markets for a turnover of Rs million*
Bangalore Division	38	89	127	3109	4.08
Bangalore (U)	02	06	08	1291	0.62
Bangalore ®	04	11	15	97	15.46
Chitradurga	04	10	14	170	8.23
Davangaere	06	08	14	334	4.19
Kolar	08	16	24	304	7.89
Shimoga	04	15	19	562	3.38
Tumkur	10	23	33	351	9.40
Mysore Division	32	46	78	1387	5.62

Chamarajnagar	03	04	07	68	10.29
Chickmagalur	05	10	15	107	14.02
Dakshina Kannada	05	03	08	330	2.42
Hassan	06	16	22	182	12.09
Kodagu	03	03	06	109	5.50
Mandya	05	09	14	228	6.14
Mysore	07	07	14	403	3.47
Udupi	03	04	07	67	10.48
Belgaum Division	48	139	187	1665	11.23
Bagaalkot	05	15	20	130	15.38
Belgaum	10	33	43	251	17.13
Bijapur	03	13	16	132	12.12
Dharwad	05	12	17	254	6.69
Gadag	05	17	22	134	16.42
Haeri	07	12	19	417	4.56
Uttara Kannada	08	27	35	240	14.58
Gulbarga Division	26	69	95	1967	4.83
Bellary	06	14	20	297	6.73
Bidar	05	09	14	158	8.86
Gulbarga	07	22	29	256	11.33
Koppal	04	13	17	616	2.76
Raichur	04	11	15	640	2.34
North Karnataka	69	198	267	3225	8.28
South Karnataka	70	135	205	4496	4.56
State Total	144	343	487	8128	5.99

Source: Government of Karnataka (2005) Karnataka at a Glance (Bangalore : Directorate of Economics and Statistics)

Agricultural marketing centers are set up to help the farmers and therefore they need honest, service minded and properly trained staff. They should be helpful to provide quick, convenient marketing services to market the agricultural produces of rural farmers. The staff of the marketing centres need to realize that the marketing network is created for extending a safety network to farmers by providing remunerative prices and helping them by removing different kinds of exploitation by the intermediaries. In the rural areas, cooperatives have to play a vital role to provide marketing services. But, cooperative societies have not come up in all rural areas of the state. Also, there is considerable unevenness in their functioning. Many of the cooperatives do not undertake the function of marketing of agricultural produces. There are different marketing societies and they need to be interwined with other societies dealing with farmers, as also providing facilities. Measures are necessary for setting up of multi-purpose cooperative societies as these societies help the farmers to get different benefits such as godowns, ware houses, transport, grading, marketing information, marketing etc., through single and convenient source.

Small and marginal farmers have their own problems in marketing of their products as their produces are very small in quantity. It is not economical for them to carry their produces to the towns; hence, village level shandies are of greater help to dispose of their produces and to get remunerative prices for their output. The State Government has developed 29 rural markets; two farmers' shandies in the state and about 10 farmers' shandies are coming. For a State of 270 towns, 29406 villages and 10401918 households the existing number of village shandies is too in adequate. Hence, there is need for developing at least one village shandy for 10 villages.

APMCs of the concerned districts and taluks need to initiate marketing measures to develop direct contact between farmers and buyers for selling food grains, pluses, fresh fruits, vegetables and greens. So that farmers could get easy marketing facilities and remunerative prices, and the buyers could get fresh items.

Concluding Remarks

The principal aim of the agricultural marketing policy should be to provide quick easy, convenient, less expensive, and profitable marketing avenues to the produces of the farmers. This is very essential on humanitarian grounds as the farmers are the working classes undergoing of physical and mental exertions. Large number of them are in helplessness position; any more exploitation will make them much more weak and put them into misery. People of civilized society should not be indifferent towards them and feel the farmers are our own brothers and sisters. It seems we have not seen much success in providing suitable marketing help to all our farmers Now, we are talking of organic cultivation to reduce the cost of production of agriculture and the second "Green Revolution". The green revolution should be successfully followed by ideal marketing revolution so that the living conditions of our farming community are going to improve in a satisfactory manner.

References

1. . Government of Karnataka (2005) 100 years of Cooperative Movement 1905 – 2005 (Bangalore : Department of Cooperation).
2. Urs, Shrijay D. (1994) Four Decades of Market Development in Karnataka (Mysore : Institute of Development Studies, University of Mysore).
3. Rao, Gopal H.S. (2000) "Experience in Agricultural Marketing in India : A Case of Regulated Markets", Southern Economist August 1, Vol. 39, No.7.
4. Government of India (2005) Economic Survey 2005 (New Delhi, Ministry of Finance, Economics Division).
5. Kohls, Richard L and Douney, David W (1972) Marketing of Agricultural Products (New York : Macmillan).
6. Thomsen, F. L. (1951) Agricultural Marketing (New York : Mc. Graw – Hill Book Company).
7. Shepherd, G.S. (1972) Marketing of Farm Products (Iowa : Iowa State University Press).
8. Abbot J.C. (1958) Marketing Problems and Improvement Programmes (Rome : FAO).
9. Government of Karnataka (2002) Report of the High Power Committee On Redressal of Regional Imbalances in Karnataka, Chairman : D.M. Nanjundappa.
10. Government of Karnataka (2005) Economic Survey 2005 (Bangalore : Planning and Statistics Department).

CHAPTER 13

Natural Resource Management in Sustainable Agriculture

The subject before us has multidimensional aspects. Unless an attempt is made to expose the sensitive issued involved in it, it becomes useless and super famous. An humble attempt is made in this paper in this direction.

Sustainable Agriculture came to be defined by many academicians in different ways. Prof M.Narasimlulu in his article "Agricultural Sustainability in India in the Context of Globalization" says that "development at present meets the needs of the present generation without compromising the ability of future generations to meet their own demand" Environmentalists look at this in terms of "balance between economic activity and environment". For some Sustainability means "trade off between the short term economic and long term well being of the society at large: As such sustainability in Agriculture means the land and other resources that are used for Agriculture to-day should be handed over to the future generation in a sustainable from so that the future generation too can continue to practice agriculture and have food security. This means the Present generations have the responsibility of exercising control over the use of all resources available in the interest of the future generation. Conservation of Natural Resources in a healthy manner for the future is the demand of the day. As such Sustainability is not merely a quantitative; it is a qualitative issue also. A look at this issue in relation to Agriculture in the Indian Context is our goal in this.

India a largely populated vast country. The Major occupation being Agriculture. Even today Agriculture is the backbone of the Indian Economy. Agriculturist is the feeder as well the protector. Days have gone back; to day we are capable of filling our bowels by ourselves rather than going with beginning bowel to other nations. We have grown to such an extent that we are able to fill others bowls in certain aspects. This sort of change over took place in a period of few decades. Production of food grains at the time of independence was 52 million tonns. Today we have got unprecedented buffer stock as well exporting food grains. Though our population is increasing. We have achieved food security. A glance at the tables given below both in the Production of food grains as well major commercial crops, makes to understand how fast the Indian farmers are.

Methododgy of the Study

The secondary data collected from different sources such has – advances estimates Ministry of Agriculture Government of India. Below tables from different publications.

Table 1: Agricultural Production- Food Grains (million tons)

Year	*Rice*	*Cereals Wheat*	*Coarse Cereals*	*Total 2 to 4*	*Pulses*	*Total Food Grains(5+6)*
1	2	3	4	5	6	7
1950-51	20.58	6.46	15.38	42.42	8.41	50.82
1955-56	27.56	8.76	19.49	55.81	11.04	66.85
1960-61	34.58	11.00	23.74	69.32	12.70	82.02
1965-66	30.59	10.40	21.42	62.41	9.94	72.35
1970-71	42.22	23.83	30.55	96.60	11.82	108.43
1975-76	48.74	28.84	30.41	108.00	13.04	121.04
1980-81	53.63	36.31	29.02	118.96	10.63	129.59
1985-86	63.83	47.05	26.20	137.08	13.36	150.44
199-91	74.29	55.14	32.70	162.13	14.26	176.39
1995-96	76.98	62.10	29.03	168.11	12.31	180.42
2000-01	84.98	69.68	31.08	185.74	11.07	196.81
2001-02	93.34	72.77	33.37	199.48	13.37	212.85
2002-03	71.82	65.76	26.07	163.65	11.13	174.77
2003-04	88.53	72.15	37.60	198.28	14.91	213.19
2004-05	83.13	68.64	33.46	185.28	13.13	198.36
2005-06AE	91.04	69.48	34.67	195.19	13.11	208.30

AE: Advance Estimates

Source: Ministry of Agriculture, Government of India.

Table 2: Agricultural Production- Major Commercial Crops (Million Tonns)

Year	Ground Nutt	Oilseeds Rapessed & Mustard	Soyabean	Total #	Sugarcane	Tea $ (Jan-Dec)	Coffee $	Cotton (Lint)@	Jute & Mesta*	Tobacco
1	2	3	4	5	6	7	8	9	10	11
1950-51	3.48	0.76	-	5.16	57.05	-	-	3.04	3.31	0.26
1955-56	3.86	0.86	-	5.73	60.54	-	-	4.18	5.39	0.30
1960-61	4.81	1.35	-	6.98	110.00	-	-	5.60	5.26	0.31
1965-66	4.26	1.30	-	6.40	123.99	-	-	4.85	5.78	0.29
1970-71	6.11	1.98	0.01	9.63	126.37	419.00	110.23	4076	6.19	0.36
1975-76	6.76	1.94	0.09	10.61	140.60	487.00	83.98	5.95	5.91	0.35
1980-81	5.01	2.30	0.44	9.37	154.25	569.60	118.65	7.01	8.16	0.48
1985-86	5.12	2.68	1.02	10.83	170.65	656.20	122.45	8.73	12.65	0.44
1990-91	7.51	5.23	2.60	18.61	241.05	720.34	169.73	9.84	9.23	0.56
1995-96	7.58	6.00	5.10	22.11	281.10	756.02	223.00	12.86	8.81	0.54
2000-01	6.41	4.19	5.28	18.44	295.96	846.92	301.20	9.52	10.56	0.34
2001-02	7.03	5.08	5.96	20.66	297.21	853.92	300.60	10.00	11.68	0.55
2002-03	4.12	3.88	4.65	14.84	287.38	838.47	275.28	8.62	11.28	0.49
2003-04	8.13	6.29	7.82	25.19	233.86	878.13	270.50	13.73	11.17	-
2004-05	6.77	7.59	6.88	24.35	237.09	982.86	-	16.43	10.27	-
2005-06AE	7.87	7.89	8.35	27.73	278.39	927.98	-	19.57	10.75	-

AE: Advance Estimate #: For nine oilseeds out of eleven in all. @ production I million bales of 170 kg. each *production in million bales of 180 kg. each

Agriculture Production - Food Grains

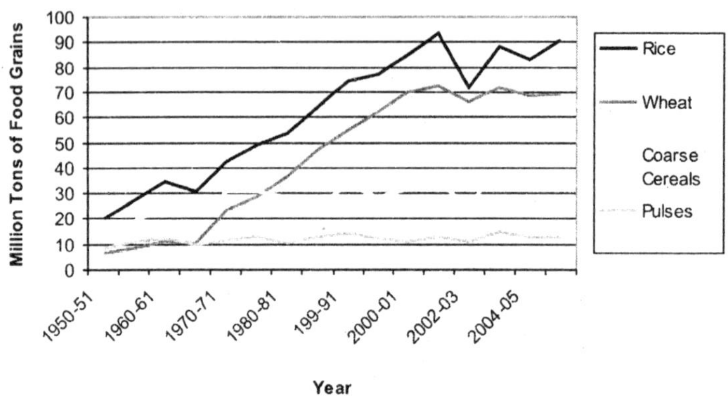

Agriculture Production Major- Commercial Crops

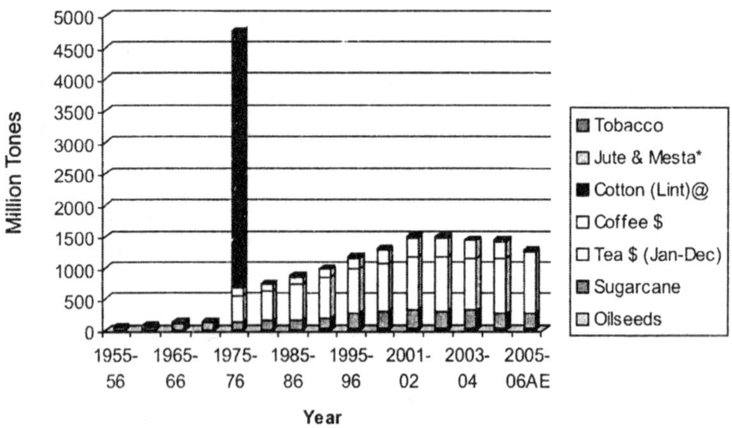

All these achievements though a necessity one has to accept because of the efforts and exercises of "Grow More Food Campaign" and "Green Revolution". Likewise we had a note worthy growth in "White Revolution" and in certain Industrial and other sectors also. But, simultaneously we have to accept the fact at what cost? It is all at the cost of extravagant, unhealthy, indiscriminate, and careless use of our natural resources. Lack of forethought landed us in a situation of unions' circle-particularly in the Agricultural sector. Medias are exposing the plight of Indian Agriculturists. In these days no day is found without a case of a suicide of farmer in one, or the other state of the nation.

The population as a whole enters in to the circle of known and unknown deceases. To quote some observations made—" A study conducted by the Chandigarh based post graduate Institute of Medical Education and Research on behalf of the Punjab Government has once again revealed that excessive use of chemical pesticides is the cause of series of deaths due to cancer in Talwadi block in Bhatinda district of Punjab." Kheti uirasat study also revealed the incidence of Cancers, Kidney failure, yellowing of teeth, Joint pain, Breathing problem, Skin disorders, on several victims. Children were marked with congenital defects like mental retardation. It also pointed out complaints of abortions, abnormal berths and Jaundice during pregnancy. Rather than elongating this aspect with a feeling that this has brought to your mind the alarming situation before us. This is the result of indiscriminate use of Chemical fertilizers, Pesticides and Fungicides-The use of chemical pesticides in 1980 was 45000tons where as at present it stands at 80000tons. In case of chemical fertilizers input, rate of increase appears formidable in these days. The table below :

Table 3: Indicates the use of Chemical Fertilisers in the Country: Fertilisers Consumption in India (NPK) in Lakh tons

Yaer	*N*	*P*	*K*	*Total*
1950-51	0.55	0.09	0.06	0.70
1960-61	2.12	0.53	0.29	2.94
1970-71	14.79	5.41	2.36	22.57
1980-81	36.78	12.14	6.24	55.16
1990-91	79.97	32.21	13.28	125.46
1999-00	116.21	48.04	17.04	181.29
2000-01	109.20	42.20	15.70	167.10
2002-03	104.70	40.20	16.00	160.90
2003-04	110.08	41.20	16.00	168.00

Source: Different volumes of Fertilizer Statistics

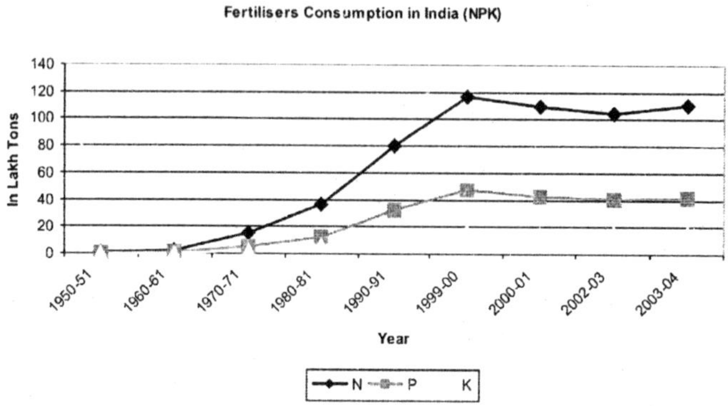

In transforming ourselves from "begging bowl to a breadbasket". We went for new verity of seeds. The Green Revolution launched by Norman Borlaug's "Miracle Seeds" on the surface appears to have brought Prosperity to Indian farmers; two decades of the Green Revolution have left the Punjab the wheat bowl of the country riddled with discontent and violence. Instead of abundance, the Punjab is best with diseased soils, pest infested crops, waterlogged deserts and indebted and discontented farmers. Instead of peace the Punjab has inherited conflict and violence. In this connection, Vandana Shiva observed "The Green Revolution has been a failure. It has led to reduced genetic diversity, increased vulnerability to pests, soil erosion water shortages, reduced soil fertility, Micronutrient deficiencies, soil contamination, reduced availability of neutrions food crops for local population, the displacement of vast numbers of small farmers from their land, rural impressments and increased tensions and conflicts. The beneficiaries have been the agro chemical industry, large petrochemical companies, manufactures of agricultural machinery dam builders and large land owners". The ambicious nature of our men at the helm of affairs put the Indian Agriculture on the Footsteps of U.S. In 1961 the Ford Foundation thus launched its intensive Agricultural Development Programme in India, intended to release "Indian Agriculture from the shackles of the past" through the introduction of Modern Intensive chemical farming. Though it is argued infavour of the results of Green Revolution lack of forethought and negligence of penetrative mood to past experience was needed but not takes care of. Because until 1960s India was usefully pursuing an Agricultural Development Policy based on strengthening the ecological base of agriculture and self-reliance of Indian peasants. Land reform was viewed as a political necessity and following independence most States initiated measures to secure tenure for tenant cultivators, to fix reasonable rents and to abolish the Zamindari system. Ceiling on land holdings were also introduced. In 1951, at a Seminar Organized by the Ministry of Agriculture, a detailed farming Strategy- The "land transformation programme" – was put forward. The strategy recognized the need to plan the bottom, to consider every individual village and sometimes every individual- field. The programme achieved major success. Indeed the rate of growth of total crop production was higher during this period than in the years following the introduction of the Green Revolution. All these went to dustbins. Recent years Governments have framed such rules and regulations to create large scale holdings to make free entry of zamindari system from the back-door in the name of liberalization, globalization and privatization, propagation of contract farming Amendments to R.M.C., free entry of Multinational Marketing agencies encouraging large holdings, Removal of all the hurdles on the way of purchase and acquition of land and farming of rules and regulations to discourage small purchase to have small holdings has largely encouraged. As a result either too pilled-up black money with politicians top bureaucrats and underworld men to pour in large amounts of money to acquire large areas of land particularly in and around urban areas of the country. These categories of people in a short period of time render the small holders land-less. As a result, in a short period of time bonded labour slavery lead to unprecedented exploitation and ultimately the poverty of a section of the society. These sections of the society in course of time migrate towards cities and towns, generating all urban problems. Totally of all these problems result in serious socio economic problems, which needs no explanation here. This is enough to show how indiscriminate uses of Agro-chemicals not only uproot the stability of Agriculture.

To bring home, how the Sustainability of Agriculture is adversely affected by using other Natural Resources, say, water both surface and underground water without any future thought.

"Indian Agriculture is a battle with Monsoon" is an old saying Mr. Schumpeter says "India lives and dies on the amount of monsoon rain". In daily weather reports, the progress of the seasonal monsoon is mapped "like an advancing battle line". It is so important to people's lives in the country. It is necessary to free the Agriculture of the country from the dependency on monsoon. The alternative available is irrigation, to provide the required water supply to Agricultural activities. In the last 40 years, efforts to boost agricultural production through irrigational projects have created an intricate system of surface canals and tube wells. Even so, Indian farmers cultivate just 43 percent of the country's potential irrigable land area. Net irrigated area has increased from 21 million hectare in 1950-51 to 55 million hectares in 1997-98 and gross irrigated area grew from 23 million hectares to 73 million hectare. Cropping intensity was 133 percent. Gross cropped area increased from 132 million hectares in 1950-51 to 191 million hectares in 1997-98. Overall cropping intensity with reference to 142 hectors of net sown area is 134 percent and is almost the same as the cropping intensity of the irrigated area. This is contrary to the expectation that multiple cropping would be more prevalent in irrigated area. The Table below shows the Net area irrigated with reference to sources of irritation and cropping intensity.

Table 4: Net area irrigated according to source(thousand hectors)

Year	*Canals*	*Tanks/ Other sources*	*Tube/ wells*	*Other wells*	*Net irrigated area*	*Gross irrigated area*	*Cropped irrigated area*	*Cropping intensity overall (%)*
1950-51	8295	6580	n.a	5978	20853	22563	108.2	111.1
1960-61	10370	7001	135	7155	24661	27980	113.5	114.7
1970-71	12838	6378	4461	7426	31103	38195	122.8	118.2
1980-81	15292	5733	9531	8164	38720	49775	128.6	123.3
1990-91	17453	5876	14257	10437	48023	63204	131.6	129.9
1995-96	17120	6585	17894	11803	53402	71352	133.6	131.8
1996-97	17262	6969	18410	12408	55049	73246	133.1	132.8
1997-98	17093	6591	18434	12448	54566	72784	133.4	134.3

n.a. =not available

Source : http://www.fao.org/DOCREP/005/ac623e/AC623Eof.htm.

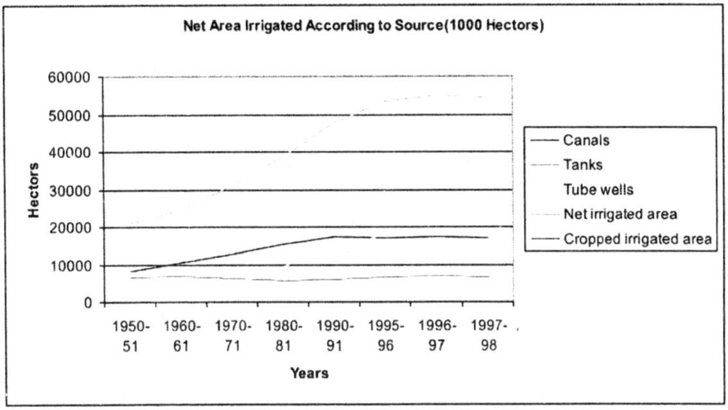

Area irrigation by cannel has steadily increased from 8 million hectares in 1950-51 to 17 million hectares in 1997-98. Irrigated area through tanks, tube wells and other wells, which are the sources of minor irrigation, increased from 13 million hectors to 37 million hectors. The share of minor irrigation in the net irrigated area is 70 percent. In order to increase Agricultural production irrigational facilities were created by the construction of dams across rivers. Tanks open-wells and other resources along with the use of ground water put together helped a lot to increase in Agricultural productivity of the country. We have to remember simultaneously to keep them in a satisfactory condition. Due to the cultivation of submerged areas of Dams and encroachment of catchments areas caused silting up of many dams and Tanks resulting in lowering the water storage capacity. Insufficient use of water from irrigation sources is not available in all seasons for multiple cropping in most irrigated areas. When it was found that surface water is not sufficient for agricultural activities Indian farmer looked towards ground water. He went on to bore the land for water. Too much extraction of the ground water; presently lead to a serious drop of ground water table. We have yet to understand how difficult it is to raise the Ground water level. Not only that to what extent the underground water reached a hazardions level. Some aquifers are contaminated with naturally occurring minerals such as arsenic, iron, sulfur and fluoride causing adverse effects on health of nearly half a million Indians. In coastal areas, salt-water intrusion from excessive groundwater pumping has also contaminated local aquifers, leaving them unusable for irrigation and human consumption.

It has been pointed out that "water pollution is a serious problem in India as almost 70 percent of its surface water resources and a growing number of its groundwater reserves are already contaminated by biological toxic organic and inorganic pollutants" (Mow R 2000). In many cases, these sources have been rendered unsafe for human consumption as well as for other activities such as irrigation and Industrial needs. This illustrates that degraded water quality can in effect contribute to water scarcity as it limits its availability for both human use and the Eco system.

In addition we have to keep in mind that water resources will strain the relationship between states with in the country and between India and neighbouring countries. This much seems to be sufficient to bring home that careful management of water resources is highly needed.

Very nearer to the prosperity of Agriculture and livestock being the Forest Wealth of the country. Inspite of emphasizing the importance of Natural Forest wealth from several points of view. Deforestation is going on to satisfy the ambitions of the present generation. Deforestation in the upper watersheds, as well as poor land management practices, have been increasing the sediment load in the rivers, while augmenting surface runoff and decreasing infiltration. More than 6000 million tons of topsoil are lost to India's rivers each year, affecting downstream hydraulics and decreasing dam capacity by an estimated 0.5 to1.2 percent annually.(World Bank 1999). This further reduces the dam's ability to store water for other purposes, there by increasing the dependence on alternative water sources such as groundwater. Decreased infiltration and dam capacity also has implications for flood control and mitigation. Water logging, salinity and alkalinity are plaguing heavily irrigated areas across the country. World Bank 1999 indicates total loss as of 1991 of Agricultural land to these factors in the country to the extent of 5.76 million hectares. It also observed that reclamation of saline and alkaline soils is expensive and difficult.

Land and pattern of its use is one of the key aspects of Agriculture. One has to consider the sustainability of Agriculture on the basis of available cultivable land. It is true its extent depends on the total land available and other factors demanded by agricultural activity. The total geographical area of India is about 329 million hectares. However the statistical is available only for 305 million hectares. The table below points out -

Table 5: The 1990-91 land utilization pattern is shown in the table below.

Land utilization pattern	*Area*	*Percentage*
i. Total Geographical area	329	-
ii. Total reported area	305	100
iii. Barren land not available for cultivation	41	13
iv. Area under Forests	68	22
v. Permanent pastures and Grazing land	12	04
vi. Cultural waste land etc	19	06
vii. Fallow lands	23	08
viii. Net area shown	142	46
ix. Area sown more than once	43	14
x. Total cropped area i.e.viii + ix	185	60

Source: Land and utilization pattern as per 1990-91 statistics made available by" Indian Agriculture in brief(Ministry of Agriculture)25th Edition of 1994.

Conclusion: Policy Implications and Results

It is indicated that the Net area cultivated appears to be 142 million hectares. Out of this Area sown more than once is only 14 percent, i.e.43 million hectares. The Net area sown is only 142 million hectares i.e. 46 percent. This includes area sown with crops and orchards. With all efforts we able to increase the area sown more than once only by 13 million hectares i.e. to 47 million hectares between 1951 and 2000.Additioan 19 million hectares or 6 percent of the total area is covered under miscellaneous trees crops such as Casuarinas trees, thatching grasses, bamboo bushes and other graves for fuel etc and cultivable wastes that lands available for cultivation but not cultivated during the previous 5 or more years due to several reasons. As a result of inadequate supply of water, Poverty of the cultivators, unremunerative farming practices, silting of rivers etc about 23 million hectares i.e.8 percent remain uncultivated temporarily for a period less than one year and not more than five years. All these put together the total area cultivable goes to-gather the total area cultivable goes to more than 200 million hectares. But the relentless growth of population, growing urbanization, ambitions Industrialization plans, formulation of Special Economic Zones, Infrastructure development etc leading to the fast disappearance of cultivable and cultivated land under concrete buildings and tare roads, even good agricultural land is being destroyed to produce bricks for construction works. In addition large areas of cultivable and cultivated even irrigated, lands available for sowing more than one crop, particularly in these days fenced as Industrial and residential plots. Political, top officers and Industrialists are grabbing thousands of hectares in urban and semi urban areas and leaving vacant with an intension of selling at higher prices in future days. The committee under the chairmanship of Ramaswamy in Karnataka recently pointed out that more than 18 thousand acres of Government land has been encroached by politicians and top officers only in two Districts of Bangalore. This sort of situation is not true only to Bangalore urban and Rural Districts; it is true even in case of other districts also. As a result the unprecedented acquisition of cultivated and cultivable land by capitalists for other purposes may push the future generation from "bread basket to begging bowl".

Rather lengthening the discussion with regard to other supporting natural resources for the sustainability of Agriculture, I wish to say in short that the Nature is bountiful but not exploit too much. Not to be too much ambition, keep in mind that future generation too has to live comfort ability. The policy makers, the bureacrates, Capitalists and other men involved in the management of Natural Resources. Keep in mind not to disturb the country's Socio-Economic, Environmental, Ecocological and Biological Equilibrium. Mis-management of Natural resources leads to misgovern of Agricultural sustainability.

References

1. .Government of Karnataka (2005) 100 years of Cooperative Movement 1905 – 2005 (Bangalore : Department of Cooperation).
2. Urs, Shrijay D. (1994) Four Decades of Market Development in Karnataka (Mysore : Institute of Development Studies, University of Mysore).

3. Rao, Gopal H.S. (2000) "Experience in Agricultural Marketing in India : A Case of Regulated Markets", Southern Economist August 1, Vol. 39, No.7.
4. Government of India (2005) Economic Survey 2005 (New Delhi, Ministry of Finance, Economics Division).
5. Kohls, Richard L and Douney, David W (1972) Marketing of Agricultural Products (New York : Macmillan).
6. Thomsen, F. L. (1951) Agricultural Marketing (New York : Mc. Graw – Hill Book Company).
7. Shepherd, G.S. (1972) Marketing of Farm Products (Iowa : Iowa State University Press).
8. Abbot J.C. (1958) Marketing Problems and Improvement Programmes (Rome : FAO).
9. Government of Karnataka (2002) Report of the High Power Committee On Redressal of Regional Imbalances in Karnataka, Chairman : D.M. Nanjundappa.
10. 10.Government of Karnataka (2005) Economic Survey 2005 (Bangalore : Planning and Statistics Department).

CHAPTER 14

The Inter-Linking Rivers Project —A Usefull Plan for Growth and Not a Mindless Dream

The interlinking of rivers is considered as the best remedy for the two recurring problems of India viz., water scarcity in the rivers of South India and the floods that affect the north Indian States. In pursuance of Supreme Court order, Government of India has set up a Task Force to consider the modalities of implementing Inter-Linking Rivers Project (ILRP) and the NDA which was in power then, declared that this task would be taken up on a war footing. The present UPA Government seems to be not much enthusiastic about this project. But Congress Party when it was in opposition during NDA Government promised that it would support this project. So, during NDA Government, more or less there was unanimity among most of political parties of India.

The idea of linking of rivers is not a new one. In the 19th Century, Colonel Sir Arthur Cotton, who is known as the father of Indian irrigation schemes was the first to coin the idea of interlinking of rivers in the country. When the East Indian Company was planning to link up different regions which were under their control with Railway tracks, Sir Cotton suggested for linking up of rivers for economical system of water transport. So Sir Cotton's prime concern was for inland navigation transport. The British Committee on Irrigation, on financial constraints grounds, dismissed the idea of linking of rivers. In 1970s, a couple of grand schemes of interlinking of rivers were proposed by Engineer / Minister K.L. Rao and Airlines Pilot Captain Dinshaw Dastur. Dr. Rao's concern was irrigation facilities and generation of electricity. Dastur's scheme was known as Garland Canal Scheme to feed Himalayan waters to the peninsular parts of the country. Rao and Dastur schemes were rejected on the grounds of their feasibility, desirability and viability. The present ILRP has been the result of estimates worked out by National Water Development Agency (NWDA).

NWDA's Proposal

The NWDA was set up in 1982 to work out basin–wise surpluses and deficits and study the storage possibilities, links and transfers The NWDA has been working on this project for over two decades and producing reports. There are three components in NWDA's project proposal, viz., The Himalayan Rivers Component (H.C) the Peninsular Rivers Component (PC) and the Hydro Electric Components. The HC envisages for a number of links, including some within the Ganga system, some between neighbouring rivers in the Brahmaputra system, a couple between those two systems, one long link from the Sarda to the Sabarmati through the Yamuna and the Rajastan, and one from the Ganga to the Subernarekha and then on to the Mahanadi. The general idea is to transfer waters to Southern Uttar Pradesh, Haryana, Punjab and Rajastan and eventually southwards to the peninsular component. The PC involves a number of links, of which the most important would be those connecting the Mahanadi, the Godavari, the Krishna, the Pennar and the Cauvery. Other links would include the Ken–Betwa, the Parbati–Kalisindh–Chambal, the Par–Tapi–Narmada and the Damanganga–Pinjal. Another idea is the partial diversion of certain rivers flowing into the Arabian sea eastwards to link with rivers flowing into the Bay of Bengal, viz., the Bedti–Varada, the Nethravathi–Hemavathi, the Pamba--Achankovil--Vaippar.

The PC will cost Rs.1,06,000 crores; the HC will cost Rs.1,85,000 crores; and the HEC will cost Rs.2,69,000. So, the total cost of NWDA project proposal will be Rs.5,60,000 crore and a 15 year deadline. According to this plan about 300 dams and more than 1000 kms of canals will be dug. Of the 30 links proposed, 14 are in the Himalayan and 16 in the Peninsular component.

Objections Raised Against ILRP

The ILRP is criticized as a mindless dream and too ambitious. The important objections raised against ILRP are given below.

1. The ILRP would flood an estimated 8000 sq kms of land and leave three million people homeless. This view is expressed

by Sudhir Vombatkere, a retired Military Engineer. According to him, this type of river linking project was thought of in Soviet Russia under Stalin regime; When rives flowing north were to be diverted to its dry central region. But even Soviet Scientists then categorically rejected the project on the pretext that it would cause enormous environmental damage.

2. Spreading of Polluted Water According to Ravi Agarwal Environmentalist of Delhi based NGO Srishti, the ILRP will spread pollution from rivers like Ganga to cleaner rivers. Inter-linking of a toxic river with non-toxic river will have a devastating impact on all of our rivers and as s result of that on all human beings and wild life. For example. Par river of Gujarat is mercury contaminated. Yamuna waters are poisonous. So when rivers are linked, pollution control will be even more difficult and many more rivers will run into sewers.
3. According to some opponents of this project, there has not been much analysis as to how flow irrigation affects soil health and river health. For instance, every river's water properties are different; and the survival of a number of aquatic species, insects and birds depends on these unique properties. Proper study has not been made on these aspects.
4. It cannot be understood now that the states that are not riparian will have no claims to the water of the rivers. Hence, a transfer of water from one region to another would be done only by consensus. But the Cauvery water dispute shows that there is simple solution to sharing river water even when the two warring states were both riparian. Since there is accord on the sharing of river water from a surplus region to a deficit one, disputes between them could increase many fold. In this context, mention may be made of Punjab state. This state has raised objection for the ILRP and earlier raised a hue and cry when desert state Rajastan as a non-riparian state was being given water from the Indus river system. There are other problems also. West Bengal, which is also objecting to the proposal fears that any linking of the Ganga and Brahmaputra might ease the flood situation in Assam, but worsen it in West Bengal.

5. The ILRP could also seriously severe india's relations with its neighbours, especially Bangladesh, which gets much of its waters from Ganga and Brahmaputra after these rivers leave our country. When India completed Farakka Barrage in the Ganga (1974) it diverted crucial dry season flows into the canals of the country. The relations between these countries have not been good since then. So far, there has been no comment from Dhaka on the ILRP.
6. The Articles on Linking of Rivers appeared in The Hindu Survey of the Environment–2003 collectively suggest that the ILRP is not an advisable project. According to Ramaswamy Iyer, it will attempt to redraw India's geography with potentially grievous results. It has been argued by Neil Pelkey that the need to pump water to a slightly higher place will make it an unrealistic project. According to Rohan D'Souza ILRP is our country's final step towards hydrological suicide. According to Biksham Gujja and Hazara Shaik the international experience with such projects does not suggest any room for optimism with the Indian experiment. Some another suggests for thinking afresh about a scheme, which assures too much on paper but actually threatens to devastate the country.
7. The costs worked out by Nilakanth Rath reveal that the ILRP needs giant amount of fund which is difficult to mobilize. Rath has worked out the likely cost of the project by taking into consideration the rate of interest at an annual rate of seven percent and the inflation rate five per cent at the end of 20 years, will come to : Peninsular Rs.3,81,878 crore + Himalayan Rs.6,66,485 crore + Hydro Electric Rs.9,69,105 crore = Rs.20,17,468 crore at the end of 20 years. Approximately, total cost comes to Rs.1,00,000 crore a year. According to Rath, it is a pity that instead of doing the first things that are crying out to be done first in regard to irrigation, people are being fed with this pie-in-the-sky type of slogan.
8. Another criticism on this project is that this project is going to benefit large number of contractors, bureaucrats, engineers, political leaders, consultants and not the water starved people of the country.

Rejoinder to the Objections

Every economic activity will be having various initial problems and oppositions. From time to time, ways and means have been worked out to over come the problems and to get more benefits. In the initial period, even machines, Air planes, Railways, Multi-Storeyed Buildings, Family Planning devices, Large Scale Industries etc., were opposed on various grounds. Now all these are accepted and have become an integral part of our life benefiting the people in many ways. Now, the ILRP is objected on various grounds. There is also point in the objections. But the benefits of ILRP are more than the problems / disadvantages. The objections raised on ILRP can be retorted as given below:

1. The first objection is on the ground that 8000 sq. kms of land is going to be flood. This may be true. This loss can be offset by providing assured irrigation facilities to millions of hectares of land in the different parts of the country. It is definitely possible to increase many times the production of agricultural, horticultural and flouricultural items in the country. There will be very wide scope for taking up animal husbandry, fishery, social forestry and other subsidiary occupations in different parts of the country. Also, there will be more scope for the generation of electricity in the country. The ILRP is proposed with the good intention of removing poverty, unemployment and improving economic welfare of millions of poor persons of the country. It is imprudent to compare foreign country experiences with Indian experiences.

2. Pollution is the fourth largest problem of Indian economy after poverty, population explosion and unemployment. Appropriate water treatment measures are needed in the cities where city effluent waters are reaching rivers. City wastes and waste waters management and treatment can be a big source of wealth for the country. By using these wastes, organic manure can be produced and sold to the farmers on commercial basis. Treated city water can be used for forestation under the highly useful social forestry programme. These measures not only keep the town and cities and rivers clean, but also help to bring about ecological

balance and increasing farm productivity in the agricultural sector. Hence, there is no point in raising objection on the ground of pollution.

3. The third one is really a silly objection. All waters of north Indian rivers are perfectly suitable to all soils of India. In no way north Indian river waters are going to affect acquatic species, insects and birds.
4. For the fourth objection – states are bound to oblige the directives of the Central Government, An Ideal National Water use policy can be formulated by the Central Government in consultation with the States and finding of ideal solution to sharing of waters is not a problem.
5. The ILRP definitely will not create any dispute with the neighbouring countries. The ILRP can utilize flood water to the maximum extent if any problems arise; they can be amicably set right through cordial negotiations. Neighbouring countries also understand that the ILRP is a human-friendly project benefiting millions of poor people of south Asian countries.
6. Regarding sixth objection – Pumping of water. No doubt, it is expensive and unwieldy. Experts may think of remodeling the scheme of ILRP in such a way as the necessity of pumping water will not arise. Side by side, ILRP also help to generate electricity in different places in sizable quantum.
7. Regarding the cost of the project. Since this project is worth while in the longer interest of the people of the country and the economic system as a whole, fund may be mobilized through people's contribution, floating of irrigation bonds, borrowing in the internal and external money markets, using of surplus funds of financial institutions etc., Regarding interest rate – interest rate alone will not rise; side by side national income will also increase when the ILRP starts to give benefits to the people of the country.
8. Regarding the eighth objection, we cannot expect charity from engineers, consultants, contractors because they are professional people; they naturally expect remuneration for their services. No doubt, there will be corruption; this can be set right by creating public opinion against corruption

on ethical grounds. If the country is prospered people will also be prospered, if the country is ruined, people of the country will also be ruined.

Rationale of Inter-Linking of Rivers

India is endowed with abundant water resources but we are not utilizing them in an economic and efficient manner. As a result of this, even now there are millions of hectares of lands are deprived of irrigation facilities, the result is continuation of poverty in the country. Owing to alarming growth of population, the demand for water and food will also increase. For this, the number of acres of land under irrigation facilities should also increase. According to one estimate, in due course of time India will overtake Peoples Republic of China, and by 2050 the population of the country would be around 150–180 crores. Therefore, it would be necessary to increase area under irrigation to 160 million hectares for all crops by 2050. The country has to evolve other strategies like diverting and usefully utilizing the excess water from one basin to another. With four percent of water resources and 15% of global population which is expected to increase to 25% by 2050, the situation will become precarious in the percapita availability of water. The percapita availability of water was 6006 cubic metres at the time of independence which is slided down to 1700 in 2004 and it is expected to fall to 1140 cubic metres by 2050. However, there will be surplus water in eastern India i.e., Brahmaputra basin and it will be 3000 cubic metres per capita. While in pennar and Sabarmati, it is as low as 300 cubic metres per capita.

Benefits are More than the Problems

Though this project is opposed on the grounds of giant cost and ecological problems, there are also large number of benefits.

I. Benefits in Agricultural Sector

The ILRP is thought of as the best plan to provide irrigation facilities to the farmers. When ILRP is completed, the living conditions of crores of poor farmers will be increased. The farmers will be able to grow two or three crops a year. Crops diversification is also possible with the availability of assured irrigation facilities. They can grow food grains, pulses, horticultural and fluoricultural crops. Subsidiary occupations such as animal husbandry, fishery, rabbits rearing, honey keeping etc., are all possible with the completion of this behemoth plan. As a result, the agricultural growth and additional employment opportunities will increase in the country. Large number of acres of lands of states like Rajastan, Madhya Pradesh, Maharastra, Andhra Pradesh, Karnataka, Tamil Nadu and other states, which were hither to, not cultivable for want of water, can be used for profitable cultivation.

2. Flood Control

India is considered as the most flood affected country in the World after Bangaldesh. The average flood flows in the Ganga and Brahmaputra are in the range of 50000 cusecs. Floods ravage North Indian states, leading to soil erosion, large scale loss of life, crops, houses of the people. The flood havocs would be minimized with the completion of the ILRP.

3. Removal of Regional Imbalances

The ILRP will also help to reduce spatial uneven economic development, and bring about permanent green revolution in the country. The backward regions of AP (Telangana), Karnataka (North Karnataka Districts), different parts of Madhya Pradesh and Tamil Nadu can be developed. The prosperity caused by supply of irrigation facilities will help for increasing welfare, happiness, peace among the people which in turn help for achieving powerful national integration.

4. Removal Poverty

Poverty in any country is among others, due to lack of opportunities. The hectic agricultural, horticultural, flouricultural activities and taking up of subsidiary occupations such as animal husbandry, fishery development, rabbits rearing, honey keeping etc., will all help to increase the living conditions of millions of farmers of rural India. The hub of activities will also help the landless to get employment opportunities around their living areas with reasonably good wages. Therefore, the ILRP can go a long way in removing poverty among the people. Besides, the forward and backward linkages of ILRP can also lead to increased employment opportunities in the country.

5. Employment Opportunities

The ILRP will help to create large number of employment opportunities for skilled/unskilled labourers, educated/uneducated unemployed persons, engineers, technicians, planners, consultants, and administrators etc. The secondary job creation effects will be in the form of growth of ancillary activities needed to supply inputs and services such as machines, transport and communication services. If, good planning and vision link this to the development of appropriate industrial and services clusters, it can be a permanent source of employment.

6. Industrial Development

Primary, secondary and tertiary sectors are all inter dependent. Development of agriculture in big way brings about various advantages to industrial sector i.e., in the form of demand for fertilizers, agricultural implements, transportation services. In the stage of development works of the ILRP, the demand for cement, iron and steel products etc., will be enormous, which in turn help for the spectacular progress in the field of industrial sector of the country.

7. Electricity Generation

Generation of electricity is one of the priority areas of our country; the ILRP will help the beneficiary states to generate more electricity than needed, and the surplus electricity can be supplied to other deficient states. This will help in compensating he imbalance caused by according special emphasis to beneficiary states. The surplus electricity can also be utilized for Railway sector, to save other sources of energy. The export sector will also benefit if electricity is available at cheaper price in adequate quantum.

8. Enormous Scope for Forestation

The 2640 km link involved with the ILRP will help for the growth of high valued and useful plants in the left and right sides of the canals. In the long run this forest resource will help to earn bigger amount of income to the national exchequer. Forestation will also help to bring about ecological balance in the country. This is compatible with Kyato Environmental Agreement.

9. Fishery Development

Construction of dams and digging of canals provide wider scope for the fishery development. There are Indian specialties like Shrimps, by increasing the production of shrimps and other marine products the country can get sizable amount of export earnings.

10. Economic Growth

The development of agriculture, industry, creation of more employment opportunities, generation of electricity will all due to the ILRP, so this project can lead to the higher growth rate of the economy. The GDP, per capita GDP will increase due to development of different sectors. On the whole, India can achieve a very high growth rate, both in the near future and distant future, due to the increased planned productive investment with a very high linkage effect.

Concluding Remarks

No doubt, the ILRP needs huge capital. Large number of acres of land is going to be submerged. Large number of trees will also fall leading to ecological damage. Large number of contractors, politicians, engineers, consultants will swallow scarce financial resources indirectly. Despite all these drawbacks, the ILRP is one of the best available giant development projects to ameliorate the poverty and unemployment problems of India. Definitely there is need for modification of the plan. Pumping of water can be avoided. Along with this plan, there is a greater need to check the flowing of waste water of cities and industries to Ganga,

Yamuna and other rivers by adapting water treatment plants in the required places. Social forestry programme is to be taken up on massive scale to facilitate the absorption of NPK elements in the waste waters of cities. Bio-manure producing plants should be set up to utilize degradable wastes. Available plastics should be used in the road construction and re–construction programmes. Glasses can be recycled for producing other glass products.

To sum up further, the ultimate aim of the ILRP is to ensure that India produces about 450 mts of food grains by 2050 when India will become number one country in the size of population. The final aim of the ILRP is to remove the problems of poverty and unemployment and to set the country in economic bloom.

References

A Report of the National Commission for Integrated Water Resources Development (1999), (New Delhi, Ministry of Water Resources, Government of India).

Ghose, Arabinad (2003), "Inter Linking of Rivers : Vision and Issues" Kurukshethan, Vol. 51, No.12, October.

Ghosh, S.N. (2002), "Linking up Rivers : A Recipe for Disaster", Mainstream 40 (52).

Gujja, Bhiskham and Shaik, Hajara (2003), "Linking of Rivers : A Systainability Perspective" The Hindu Survey of the Environment – 2003.

Iyer, Ramaswmay R (2003), "Linking Rivers; A Chimera of a Project" The Hindu Survey of the Environment – 2003 (Chennai : The Hindu).

Pelkey, Neil (2003), "Linking Rivers : Cost of the Behemoth" The Hindu Survey of the Environment–2003.

Pillai, Karunakaran G (2004), "Inter Linking of Rivers in India" The IEA 87th Conference Volume, The Indian Economic Association.

Prabhu, Surnesh (2003), Inter Linking of Rivers in India, Press Information Bureau, Government of India.

Prasad, HAC (2002), "Ganga – Cauvery Rink : A Master Plan for Growth, (Chennai : The Hindu Business Line).

Rao, K.L. (1971), India's Water Wealth (New Delhi; Orient Longman Ltd.).

Rath, Nila Kanta (2004) "Linking Rivers : Some Elementry Arithmetic" EPW Vol. XXXVII, No.29.

Vombatkere, S.G. (2003), Inter Linking: Salvation or Folly II, India Together, January.

CHAPTER 15

Agrarian Distress and Alleviatory Measures

Abstract

At the outset, I wish to say a few words about the paper. This is a critical analysis of the subject. It is based on observations made by leading authors, supported by secondary data. Coming from rural area that too from an Agricultural family, I have a closer view of the Agricultural sector and Agriculturists. As a teacher in Economics I have Historical and Theoretical knowledge of the subject. Therefore it is a synchronization of theoretical as well a pragmatic approach with a critical touch.

India a vast and highly populated Economy. Its natural resources cannot be said as scarce. The vast land and the large human resource if properly being used Indian Agriculture will be in the fore- front in the world economy. But the condition of Agriculture in the country is not encouraging, low yield, unsecured price, burden of loan, traditional and superstitious practices, exploitation by middlemen and ignorance of law leading to exploitation by Government machinery, etc are at the base to put the Agricultural sector on the cross-road – ultimately lead to the distress – wide spread suicides of farmers. This is totally the make up of our policy makers, Government personnel from bottom to the top who always read and interprets the rules and regulations between the lines and between the letters to the detrimental of the farmers. In certain regions of the country particularly in Karnataka it appears that the policy makers, personnel of the Government machinery, Industrialists, men with large amounts of block money and gangs of Land Memphian have came together, made such rules and regulations to get ali the Agricultural land in to their own grip. Karnataka is a state that one can purchase thousands and thousands of acres easily but no one can purchase one or two acres of land easily. A small purchaser hearts to be an Agriculturist whatever his education may be will not be allowed on the prefix of one or the other reason. Any persistence costs several thousand in the from of bribe. Diagnosis reasons for this plight of Agricultural sector of the country will lead us to search for the solutions. To find solutions are the measures to alleviate the problems faced by the sector only requires a will and open-minded honest approach by our policy makers and the Government personnel concerned. The persons who call themselves as thinkers and Agricultural Economist, Agricultural Scientists, etc without hesitation or without any desire for favour from our policy makers came out with their observations. Such a co-ordinated and willful approach will be the only possible way to put the Agriculture on the right read to progress. Not mere lipsimpathy about the Indian farmers. My paper though not at length, is an attempt to touch the aspects which one more important.

Introduction

India a country with huge population. It is second in the size of population. The population projections indicate that the size of population by 2021 is expected at 1,345 million with a growth rate of 1.44 percent per annum. Expecting an average growth rate at o.68 percent per annum between 2021 and 2051 the size of population would be around 1,646 million. Though appears to be alarming a clear study of the resources of the country it ids not so much distressful.

Geographically India is a vast country. It measures 3214 KM from North to South and 29933km from east to west i.e. with an area 32,87,782 Sq,km bounded by Hindukush Himalayan mountain – ranges at the North, which is a Defence against the Northern side as well a perennial source of water for the North Indian, South East and West surrounded by water. These features really cut at our Defence expenditure, Plans of utilization of Northern rivers for Southern part of the country and to facilitate the progress of Agriculture of the country remains still on papers.

The size of population is not a curse. It is a source of means for Economic development. The Human resources depended on the size of population, whatever the Natural Resources that a country is endowed with unless suitable Human Resources is available economic development is a misnearer. We have human power in abundance but it is not converted in to human resource suitable for the Economic Development . Human Resource planning – suitable education, training , building up of required expatriation for the future is yet to be thought of. As a result an army of unemployed is expanding resulting in the coming up of all sorts of social evils in the country.

In addition, India is in possession of other resources – water, power, mineral, favorable climate, etc – all put to-gather too, there is a saying, " India is a rich country, with poor people". However inspite of its multi – religion, lingual, cultural and traditions , it is a strong Democracy able to influence and direct the world economic policies. It is essential to look to the out –comes of the economy including the Agricultural sector and its states as well its plight in these days. The present situation of Agricultural sector and the Agriculturists is not sudden occurrence. It is the mistakes and misleading unforesighted policy results put – together ultimately lead to the widespread distress in the Agricultural sector leading to suicides of farmers not only in the dry-land belt but also in fertile and resource – endowed regions.

Importance

We have to remember the peculiar nature of Indian farmers before going in to the analysis of the centre of the subject. Agriculture in India is not merely an occupation it is a way of life to farmers. The deep rooted cultural and religions habits of the farmers made them to develop a sentimental attachment to land. Land is everything to every farmers. Let us analyze the different aspects of Indian Agriculture to diagnose the reasons for this state of affairs of agricultural sector.

Agriculture is the edifice of the Indian Economy. It is the keystone in the structure of Economic Development of the country. It is a sources of food, fodder, raw – materials etc in the economy. It is the fuel for the running wheels of the Industrial sector.

In short we may quote Prof Kuznets as he identifies four possible types of contributions that the Agricultural sector is capable of making to overalls Economic Development :

1. Product contribution, i.e. making available food and raw materials.

2. Market contribution i.e. providing the market for producer goods and consumer goods produced in the non-agricultural sector.
3. Factors contribution i.e. making available labour and capital to the non-agricultural sector and
4. Foreign Exchange contribution.

India is the 7th largest land-owner in the world after Russia, Canada, China, the U.S.A., Brazil and Australia. In terms of percentage India has just 2.4 percent of the world surface with a population around 109 cores. The area of land available has to used with more care keeping in mind the future economic facts. The 1990-91 land utilization pattern is shown in the table below.

Table 1: The 1990-91 land utilization pattern

Land utilization pattern	*Area*	*Percentage*
i. Total Geographical area	329	-
ii. Total reported area	305	100
iii. Barren land not available for cultivation	41	13
iv. Area under Forests	68	22
v. Permanent pastures and Grazing land	12	04
vi. Cultural waste land etc	19	06
vii. Fallow lands	23	08
viii. Net area shown	142	46
ix. Area sown more than once	43	14
x. Total cropped area i.e.viii + ix	185	60

The table makes it clear that out of the total reported land area of 305 million hectares, net area sown is only 142 million hectares or 46 percent of the total land area. The partition of the country necessitated massive measures to achieve self-sufficiency in food. As a result various " Grow More Food" programmes initially aimed at increasing the net cultivable area in the country. This was done by turning grazing lands and forest lands into croplands, shifting waste land into cultivation, changing cropping pattern in such a way as to divert land under fodder crops to other crops and so on. Thus till the beginning of 1960s. The increase in Agricultural production was more the result of expansion of cropped area. This kind of extensive agriculture is no longer to continue. The National Commission on Agriculture made it clear in 1976 that the net area shown could increase only marginally say up to 145 million hectares by 2001. To some extent, these factors have generated some positive influences on Agriculturists. But later on the net shown area could actually declined, with the relentless growth of population and growing urbanization – Cultivated and Cultivable land is fast disappearing under Concrete buildings, widening and formation of 'New Tare Roads', and also good agricultural land is being destroyed to produce bricks for construction of houses and other buildings. When the expansion of area under cultivation started dwindling, the plight of marginal farmers slowly started moving towards difficulties.

On the other as per the census of 2005 population size demanded an increase of food grains by 250 and more million tonns. Though India can meet the challenge as it has wasteland, water and sunlight resources. Reality is something different. Most of the land remained uncultivated i.e. underutilized, unirrigated, single cropped and low- yielding. The possibility of increasing the country's irrigated area is vast efforts appears to be less. However, multiple cropping, and the area sown more than once had increased from 13 million hectares to 47 million hectares between 1951 and 2000. Yet there is a vast scope for double cropping, other allied agricultural activities, rural Agri – based industries, diversification cropping as open the demands of the day, speedy implementation of irrigational programmes, Institutional credit, Administrative misleading and growing mismanagement of our soil, etc naturally lead to disappointments among the Agriculturists. This became more clear by a look at the comparative yield of different countries in different crops with ours. This indicates that the agricultural productivity is possible to be increased even without extending mere physical area under the plough.

Table 2: Actual yield per hectare in quintals in 1999.

	Potential of high yielding Indian varieties	*Actual yield in India*	*Actual yield of the world's largest producer*	*Country*	*world's highest yield*	*Country*
Food crops	-	-	-	-	-	-

Rice(paddy)	40 to 58	29.5	63.2	China	88.8	Egypt
Wheat	60 to 68	25.8	39.7	China	80.5	UK
Maize	60 to 80	16.7	83.9	U.S.A.	96.9	Italy
Non-food Crops	-	-	-	-	-	-
Sugarcane	-	680	686	Brazil	1,190	Egypt
Groundnut (pods)	20 to 30	9.1	27.9	China	30.4	U.S.A.
Cotton (Lint)	15 to 20	2.3	10.2	China	12.7	Australia
Jute	25 to 30	200	20.0	India	25.2	China

Problems, Solutions

In the case of rice, the highest yield in the world is nearly 89 quintals per hectare recorded by Egypt. In case of wheat, the highest yield recorded by England i.e. over 80 Quintals per hectare. China, which is the single largest producer of both rice and wheat in the world, records an average of 63 quintals and 40 quintals per hectare respectively. If we take into consideration the potential Annual yield, the gap between the actual yield and potential yield in all our crops and the gap between the average yield in India and the average yield in many countries of the world pose a challenge and an opportunity for India to increase its production. All theses facts points out that agricultural productivity in the country though average yield per hectare has shown an development but the full potential has to be realized. Though some improvement is seen during the plan period the conditions in Agriculture have not changed much. The challenges, still becomes more glaring by a comparative study with the size of growing size of population, rural employment, conditions of marginal agriculturists and landless etc. I have narrated all these aspects only to show that the increase in agricultural production to some extent make our Agriculturists to have hopes for the future. When he finds himself as the state of stagnation with regard to the size of productivity inspite of his efforts moves him to loose heart this is what happen in the past few months, particularly with regard to small farmers. It is high time to rectify us and to go to the rescue of our farmer by diagnosing the reasons for low productivity in the Agricultural sector and to find the measures to over-come. The factors responsible for this state of affairs of the Indian agriculture may conveniently grouped under three heads a) General factors b) Institutional factors c)Technological factors

a. General factors

The real problems of Indian agriculture are that there is too many people who depend on agriculture. Since 1901 the proposition of people depend on this sector has all most remained constant say around 70 percent. This sort of over-crowding and consequent pressure of population on land has lead to sub- division and fragmentation of holdings, decline in the area of land percapita, disguised unemployment and marginal productivity of labour, which may be zero or even negative. Inspite of the exposition in acreage, the pressure of population on land has been so heavy that between 1901 and 2001 the area of cultivated land percapita has declined from 0.43 hectare to 0.20 hectare. This really needs measures to reduce the pressure on land. Several measures are possible to be thought over in these regard. Rural industria-lization is one possible way. Agro based Industries are possible to established. Allied agricultural activities like poultry, sleep breeding and raring, piggery, diary farming, floriculture, horticulture, fish culture, and food processing etc are these which absorb the excess population on land. Not only the big farmers, even the marginal once also find a way of earning in addition to their agricultural activity. Suitable training to farmer in these areas will attract them to take-up. In certain states such schemes have been evolved but not effective steps have been taken. The machinery, which has to implement these must have a positive look and a zeal and commitment to do something positive to the farmers. Since many years these measures have not yielded the expected results. Here budget allocation will not be fruitful, it is the end result what is necessary. In addition effective policy measure are to be formed and executed to check the growth of rural population. Suitable education in this regard needs importance. When all these are push together and implemented with commitment. With an aim to do positive to the rural flock, Indian farmer in a addition to his agricultural activity he will find himself in a highest income level which makes him more confident and capable of overcoming his short-comings. Every body knows who's responsibility is this.

i) Discouraging Rural Atmosphere

The Indian former generally are poor, illiterates, ignorant, superstitions, conservation and bounded by outmoded customs and institutions such as the caste system and the joint family. Superstition and belief in fate are the curses which keep the farmers fully satisfied with their primitive system of cultivation except for a small group of enlightened farmers, who adopt modern techniques of production, vast majority of farmers are not motivated by consideration of economic progress.

Are the above are unsolvable ones? Certainly not. Even though we have crossed ½ a centaury since Independence having our own government and our own people at all level of government the situation moved very little. Every year in the budget speeches, it is heard very many projects have been launched. What is the result? I think what we have noticed in the past few months. Suitable education to the farmers on the lines of modern and scientific cultivation is yet to reach him. Even the children in the rural areas do not have proper primary education. Single teachers schools, teachers engaged in their personal business, unsupervised schools, schools under trees and in temples are not uncommon. This state of affairs to a great extent lead to illiteracy and ignorance. Rich and the well to do land owners moves out their children to cities and towns for education. Left over are poor not able to meet the cost of city and town schools. So poor farmers remains poor to years to come.

One more purposeful policies are being put to operation to keep educated and progressive minded people out of Agriculture on the private providing purchase of agricultural land fights only to Agricultural family members who owns land already or who had an inherited landed property. Any one other than this will not be allowed to purchase. IT is only possible when he obtains permission from revenue authorities of certain rank. This sort of regulatory measures certainly keep the educated, progressive minded ones, interested to be in village, embracing agriculture as their living. This type of regulatory measures have already lead to rampant corruption, land maphias in the concerned departments. People at the top government officers of highest ranks, some industrialists in many cases supported by people from under-world are purchasing agricultural lands in thousands of hectares. This ultimately lead to the diversion of Agricultural lands from Agriculture to formation of New-town-ships, Resorts, Luxurious hotels, in few cases Floriculture, Poultry, Piggery farms. This type of activity appears too common around 50-60kms around cities like Bangalore, Mysore, Mangalore, Hassan, and Mandya etc. This sort of taking so much of fertail agricultural land is unwarranted, when 50% of the plots and houses in these cities are vacant. It appears very clear even to a layman, that these people are purchasing these lands as high stakes to find a way for their large quantities of black money. Some industrialists garbed the large areas of land to sell it later at high prices as to build flats and hotels. In certain cases even the lands in rural areas too going in to the hands of these people in thousands and thousands of hectares. This, in a way the entry of Neo-Zamindars system. In the later days if this trend is not abated early farmers particularly the small farmers will fall in to hot waters. The trend in future is more cruel compared to the then existed Zamindari system. How it is happening? With who's support? Why such regulatory measures were framed? All these questions need no explanatory answers as it known to one and all. Big ones with bagful of currencies are given red carpet welcome to all activities in our government officers. But a poor farmer has to suffer many months for trivial matters. Here I wish to point out a case to bring home how the things are taking shape in these days. (This is in Karnataka) A post graduate after coming to a definite decision to move to a rural area and to take up agriculture for his livelihood out of few thousand rupees left –over by his future. He decided to purchase a hectare of land suitable for cultivation. When he came to know that he has to obtain a permission to purchase such a land he went directly to the concerned officer of the Revenue department. The officer concerned after so many visits directed him to an another officer like-wise this went for a few months. Everyone took as much as possible from him however as last a certificate of permission was obtained but where is the money to purchase the land whatever he had for the purpose went in to the purses of these officers. Ultimately a young post- graduate finding himself in state of helplessness breathed last.

This young educated even understanding the aims and goals of the present rules and ruralers would have joined hands with the groups who have Gulls and Guns to oppose this state of affairs. My question is such a regulatory measures are warranted/Governments are not capable of avoiding Agricultural land moving in to the hands of Capitalists businessmen. Government officers, Politicians in thousands of hectares. But putting all hurdles for a small purchases that too for his livelihood. Why such things taken are happening? Who are responsible for such affairs? We boost ourselves saying that we are for the upliftment of Agriculture and farmers. Is this the way? Solutions are needs no explanation – Primary education is more than enough to chalks out the projects, programmes, measures to over-come these evils.

ii) Inadequate Non-farm –Services

Indian agriculture is suffering from the non-existence of Non-farming services like – Institutional finance, market information and facilities, and lack of cold storage, Go-down facilities, price guarantee, Insurance against crop failure due to natural factors, Insurance facilities for livestock,etc. In certain regions such facilities are being in existence very scanty. There also the small farmers are left at the mercy of middlemen and officers. Who is to bell the cat?

b) Institutional Factors

i) Size of Holdings:

The size of holdings in India is very low, less than two hectares or five hectares. Not only Agricultural holdings are small, they are fragmented and subdivided too. This is going to be intensified by the present regulatory measures of the government as already pointed out leading to many other negative effects. Unsuitability scientific cultivation on the one hand and on the other waste of time , labour, cattle power, proper utilization of irrigational facilities, quarrels and litigations among farmers consequently low yield per hectare resulting in the intensification of poverty, situation requires only suitable measures for consolidation of holdings. The early measures on ceiling on land holdings have been thrown in to dustbins in one of the other names- may be urbanization, Industrialization, Special sectors for economic growth etc. Say that in the name of urbanization, In cities and towns(particularly corporation and District head quarters) nearly

30 to 50 percent of the vacant developed housing plots are remaining unutilized the concerned Developing authorities permitting private Builders and Developers undertake the formation of New lay-outs taking large areas of agricultural land in to their hold. In the name of Industrialization some industrialists have acquired lands only to compound them. The government of India in the name of EPZ & lakhs and lakhs of acres of Agricultural land go in to the hands of some dominating Industrialists. In this connection we may just say a sort of Real Estate Deal. Even in Real Development activities such a thing is already much came in public discussions. By spending lots and lots of Tax payers money our policy makers are very eager to provide land ownership to capitalists or combination of politicians and government officers in the name of special projects for Economic Development rendering our farmers poor and poorer. Is it difficult to identify the people involved for all these evils ?. But who is to Bell the Cat?

c) Technological Factors

Old and traditional methods of cultivation are common. Scientific and modern methods of cultivation, using improved techniques and tools is not known to Indian farmers improved seeds proper and adequate managing, using of pesticides, economical use of water, mechanization are all less known to Indian Agriculturalists lack of knowledge and guidance, less purchasing power are the major bottlenecks in this direction. The subsidized supply of improved seeds, modern tools and machineries go in to the hands of big and influential farmers and middlemen. Real needy ones are generally left-out. This situation is known in general without any efforts to rectify. Importing knowledge about modern methods of cultivation to farmers and adequate advisory facilities at the farm level knowledge is yet to make its appearance. Agriculture is an activity concerned with plant -- life; It is not an Arm-chair along with A.C. chambers life people involved must come out of A.C chambers and go to each and every land cultivated and advise the farmers for any lapses. Agricultural scientists and the Extension service personnel has to understand this and Act. Is it difficult to understand the responsibility of ratification of the situation?

ii) Inadequate Irrigation:

The basic weakness of Indian Agriculture is the inadequate irrigational facilities. The irrigated land is only 33 percent out of the total available under the plough. Construction of new dams for perennial Rivers, renovation and de-silting of tanks, reinforcement and proper utilization of Groundwater, importing sound and necessary knowledge to farmers in using water etc are the early requirements to put our Agricultural sector on proper Road of progress.

What is observed in the paper is just a summarized picture, However, it throws a light on the responsibility, and efforts required from an corners to Alleviate Agrarian distress to inflict conference among our farmers.

References

Economic Survey Government of Karnataka, 2005-06, Bangalore.

Statistical abstract of Karnataka (2006), 2000-01, Directorate of Economics and Statistics, Bangalore. http.www.yahoo.com. Http.www. google.com

CHAPTER 16

Contract Farming in India

Abstract

Indian Economy is an Agricultural Economy. Agriculture is the pivot around which the economic activity of the country revolves round. This sector is the source of food, fodder, and raw-materials. It is not merely an occupation but the life of Indian Population. The progress is otherwise of the agriculture is the determinant of social, economic, and political status of the country. On the background of expanding demand for food products and raw materials, it is necessary to reutilize the sector. From time to time landforms, methods of cultivation, marketing management, processing techniques of agricultural products etc. have been modified to meet the demands of the day. With the emergence of free trade in the wake of Globalization of the economy, the entire economic activities of the country came to be exposed to tough competition. To withstand the situation arising out of this "Contract Farming" is one of the best-suggested mechanisms, added to this, to uplift the status of Agricultural Community of the country.

Contract Farming is often confused because there are so many different contracts and sectors i.e. private sector firms, public sector companies, international agencies have entered into the field. However, 'Contract Farming' can be defined as and agreement between farmers and processing and/ or marketing firms for the production and supply of agricultural products under a forward agreement generally as permitted prices. The agreements also allow the purchaser to provide a degree of production support through inputs and technical guidance for the crop cultivation. From the farmer's side there is commitment to produce the specified agricultural produce within the specified quality and quantity standard prescribed by the purchaser and the purchases commits him to purchase the product as an agreed price. To be in short 'Contract Farming' is a "grow to order way of farming that facilities easy access to millions of farmers for an assured and organized production, processing, marketing and credit linkages to usher in Green Revolution II in India".

Contract Farming has wider scope in India. The wide available Cultivable Geographical Area in the country provides for multiple crop cultivation, climatic diversities in different regions of the country also helps to grew verities of products and also to undertake various allied activities closely connected to farming. As the Cultivator and Corporate/ Firms/Individuals engaged in processing and marketing of Agro and Agro-related products comes to-gather through an agreement. Cultivator under this system is assured of the price for the quantity of the product what he grows subject to the quality of the product. One firm which has entered in to the agreement looks after the guidance with regard to method and technical know-how and other inputs such as Supply of Seeds, Fertilizers, Pesticides, Fungicides, Marketing and other input items. As a result, the cultivator will be able to cultivate with confidence without worrying himself for capital investments for inputs for cultivation. The assured price after the harvest provides the cultivator economic stability there by it infuse confidence in his activities. Under this system cultivator is free from price fluctuations and market hazards and exploitation by intermediaries and bureaucrats. This is what highly needed to protect the cultivator at present. This system has long-term benefits for both growers and purchaser if their long-term association is mutually complimentary.

In India, a sizable part of the community falls under the small and marginal farmers' category. Therefore, Contract Farming becomes increasingly important as it allows their agricultural produce to be purchased by multinationals, Government Agencies, Small Compinies, Farmers' Co-operatives and Individual Entrepreneurs. Many states in the country particularly Andra Pradesh, Karnataka, Chattisgarh, Haryana, Madhya Pradesh, Maharastra, Punjab, Rajasthan, Tamilnadu,Uttarkhand and Uttra Pradesh have provided favorable conditions for the spread of contract farming. Recent studies too have indicated the possibilities of expansion of contract farming in the country. New

Corporate/Firms/Individual Entrepreneurs are also entering into this field. Agricultural Community is also exhibiting its willingness to enter into agreement with one or other firms involving one or more products.

Objectives and Methodology

In this context an attempt is made in the present study focus on benefits of contract farming to the farmers, company/firm and for both and then farmers' perception on contract farming, to identify the strategies which are useful to improve contract farming and finally what are all the steps has to be taken by the government for the development of contract farming. The study based on the secondary data.

A deep look into the practical side of contract farming in the country. An experience differs from individual farmers to farmers and Firms/Companies to Firms/Companies, Many farmers, Firms, and Companies as well some scholars claim various advantages in favour of contract farming. However, it is not possible to deny some disadvantages of contract Farming. It is suggested that suitable steps are to be taken to formulate policies with regard to the shortcomings of the contract agreements. Particularly relating to the specificity, enforcement aspects, conservation of soil nutrients, and protection against over-usage of chemical fertilizers, pesticides, and Fungicides etc. The future of Contract Farming in the country depends upon the transparency and the enforcements aspects of the Contract Agreement between Firms/Companies/Entrepreneurs and Farmers entering into such Contracts.

Introduction

Indian economy is predominantly an agricultural economy. Agriculture is the main source of Food, Fodder and Raw materials. Agriculture is a major contributor to the National Revenue also. In short, the economic activities revolve round around the pivot. Agriculturists of the country have not merely taken this as an occupation but a way of life. Their bondage with land is so inseparable. Every one in the country desires to and aims at owning some price of land in his life time. It has been to some extent considered a matter of social status. In spite of this India is not very free from worries with regard to agricultural commodities. Compared to developed countries its productivity in this sector is not fully satisfactory. One has to accept that the productivity per hector in respect of certain crops is far below. In the light of increasing population it is highly necessary to suitable the agricultural sector. Since independence, modifications, and experiments went on with regard to unit of holding, unit of cultivation, methods of cultivation etc in the name of land reforms, scientific cultivation, intensive cultivation etc. With this though achievements were noteworthy but not to the extent desired. Due to the demands of the day, we launched Green Revolution.

During the period of Green Revolution, several facilities were extended to cultivators. Several policies and regulations were enacted to push-up agricultural sector. The increasing demands for agricultural products necessitated us to step in to Green Revolution II. Tough competition in the market due to Liberalization, Privatization, and Globalization. Agricultural sector of the country has to be protected from the on slats of market forces in the name of infrastructure development. Industrialization and Urbanization, the doors of legislation were kept opened for capitalists to grab even cultivable land in to their hold, which is paving the way for dwindling the area of land under the plough. Hence, it is highly necessary to find a way to increase agricultural productivity and to lift the agricultural community to a tolerable economic status. In the light of these facts, 'contract farming' came to be accepted as one of the attractive methods of cultivation by the cultivators at present.

Definitions of Contract of Farming

"Contract farming is defined as a system for the production and supply of agricultural and horticultural produce under forward contracts between producers and buyers. The essence of such agreement is the commitment of the producer to provide an agricultural commodity of certain types, at a time and price, and in the quality required by a known and committed buyers. Buyers engaged processing and marketing agricultural products are entering into contracts with the farmers. They provide the farmers with the inputs and buy back the product with a rate specified in advance".

To be more explanatory 'contract farming' can be defined as an agreement between farmers and processing/or marketing firms for the production and supply of agricultural products under a forward agreement, generally at pre- determined price. The agreement also allows the purchaser to provide a degree of production support through inputs and technical guidance for the crop cultivation. From the farmer's side, there is a commitment to produce the specified agricultural products with in the quality and quantity prescribed by the purchaser, in turn farmer's production, and purchases the produce. In nutshell 'contract farming' is a 'grow to order' way of farming that facilitates easy access to millions of farmers for an assured and organized production, processing, marketing and credit linkages to ushers in Green Revolution II in India.

In India, 'contract farming' has wider scope. Contract farming is practiced in various crops. The wide available cultivable geographical area in the country provides ample scope for multiple crop cultivation, climatic diversities of the country also helps to undertake various allied activities closely related to farming. Under this system farmer is freed from capital input worries such as seeds, machinery and tools for agricultural activities. Fertilizers, Pesticides, Fungicides, etc. Technical guidance for cultivation too is being provided by contracting firms/ companies/individual entrepreneurs. As the purchase price is guaranteed cultivator need not worry about the price fluctuations and any market hazards and malpractices. As a result, farmers under this system are secured and safe largely.

Objectives and Methodology

In this context an attempt is made in the present study focus on benefits of contract farming to the farmers, company/firm and for both and then farmers' perception on contract farming, to identify the strategies which are useful to improve contract farming and finally what are all the steps has to be taken by the government for the development of contract farming. The study based on the secondary data.

Government Policy, Different Companies and Crops

With the declaration of the Government of India's 'National Agricultural Policy' which envisages - "Private sector participation will be promoted through contract farming and land leasing arrangement to allow accelerated technology transfer, capital inflow and added to this the liberalization of seed policy has enabled the import of new varieties of crops, both Hybrids and High -yielding by corporate bodies through joint ventures. Being attracted by the long-term benefits by new policies a number of multinationals, small companies, government agencies, farmers' cooperatives and individual entrepreneurs entered in the system. To mention a few pioneer originations in the field are - Rallies, Appachi cotton. PepsiCo, Ghekin promoted companies about more than 25 in numbers, UgarsugarLTD, Dunakiliti Konzervuzeu KPT, Unicorn, Agro-tech LTD, Lutergarden (India) Pvt. LTD, etc. The process of entering into the fold of this system by new organizations/ companies is increasing day by day. As this system of agriculture and allied activities is expanding, many crops are also coming into this field. The crops grown were mostly coconut, arecanut, paddy, ragy, groundnut, sunflower, vegetables, banana, barley, gherkin ,onion, tomato, watermelon, sweet melons, capsicum, chilies, beans, peas, carrot, baby corn, popping corn, gram, some medical plants, chicken rearing both boilers and hatches etc.

Contract Farming - Different States in India

Because of some favorable conditions such as lower total land under marginal fields, better irrigation facilities, soil productivity and yield per hectare, contract farming is expanding in India particularly in states such as Andhra Predesh, Karnataka, Haryana, Madhya Pradesh, Maharastra, Punjab, Rajastan, Tamil Nadu, Uttarkhand , Uttar Pradesh and Chettisgarh.

History of Contract farming in Karnataka: A Brief Note

The practice of contract farming was prevalent in the sugar industry where farmers agreed to grow sugarcane at a pre-notified price for decades. Of late, MNCs have entered into the agricultural sector and introduced a number of horticultural crops, and their products have a high demand in international markets. Contract farming, as it existed then, was different from the design and functioning of contract farming methods obtaining today. In other words, the state notifies the price and extends other facilities i.e., supply of seeds, fertilizers, package of practices, and buy-back from the farmer's field, grade-wise fixation, and, more importantly stands guarantee for the contract agreement between the farmer and the concerned MNCs. The liberlisation of seed policy has enabled the import of new varieties of crops, both hybrids and high yielding, by corporate bodies through joint ventures.

Karnataka's agrarian structure is very conducive in promoting contract farming in the country. The distribution of number and area of operational holdings across gender and major size classes during 1995-96 and 2000-01 is given in Table No-1. The aggregate pattern of percentage variation in the number of operational holdings and the area operated by size class reveals 13.8 percent and 1.6 percent respectively in the 1995-96 and 2000-01 agricultural census. In other words, the number of operational holdings was increasing, while the area operated was decline during the successive agricultural census in the state. It is interesting to note that across all size classes the percentage variation in the medium and large holding categories negative trends. Further, the percentage variation in the operational holdings (Male & Female) increased by 14 percent and 27 percent respectively between 1995-96 & 2000-01. Whereas, percentage variation of female area operated has increased by 14 percent, while the corresponding figure for male operational holdings shows negative (-0.2percent) percentage variation in the state. It is noteworthy that both the number of operational holdings and area under operation among marginal and small farmers categories have shown increasing trend during the reference period.

Karnataka will shortly emerge as one of the Food Park Centers in the food basket of India. Within a short span of time, Karnataka may see billionaires not only in the IT sector but also in agriculture in general, and, in particular, in the food processing segment of the above sector. The Karnataka agro-food processing industry is all set to put the state in the world map: with six parks ready for take off as public-private partnerships, the state is ushering India into the multi-billion dollar international market.

Table. 1 Distribution of Number and Area of Operational Holdings according to Sex & Major Size, Classes

Size Class	Number of holdings (in 000)							Area operated (in 000" hectares)						
	2000-01			1995-96				2000-01			1995-95			
	Male	Fe-male	T*	Male	Fe-male	T*	% of Variation	Male	Fe-male	T*	Male	Fe-male	T	% of Vari-ation
Marginal (1ha)	2630 (44)	616 (54)	3252 (46)	2154 (40)	452 (50)	2610 (942)	24.6	1217 (11)	273 (17)	1492 (12)	1039 (10)	208 (15)	1248 (10)	19.6
Small (1-2ha)	1623 (27)	283 (25)	1909 (27)	1473 (28)	232 (26)	1707 (27)	11.8	2333 (22)	404 (25)	2742 (22)	2143 (20)	335 (24)	2480 (21)	10.6
Semi Medium (2-4 ha)	1095 (19)	162 (14)	1259 (18)	1062 (20)	11 (16)	1204 (11)	406	2984 (28)	439 (27)	3429 (28)	2912 (27)	383 (27)	3298 (27)	4.0
Medium (4-10ha)	504 (9)	64 (6)	569 (8)	534 (10)	59 (7)	594 (10)	-4.2	2942 (28)	366 (23)	3317 (27)	3138 (30)	345 (24)	3490 (29)	-5.0
Large (10ha)	79 (1)	9 (1)	90 (1)	96 (2)	10 (1)	106 (2)	-15.1	1149 (11)	134 (8)	1327 (11)	1419 (13)	142 (10)	1593 (13)	-16.7
All sizes	5931 (100)	1134 (100)	7079 (100)	5319 (100)	894 (100)	6221 (100)	13.8	10625 (100)	1616 (100)	12307 (100)	10651 (100)	1413 (100)	12109 (100)	1.6

P/V: Percentage Variation. Note: * Figures also includes number & area of institutional holdings, which are neglible, Figures within brackets are percentage to the column totals

Source: Agricultural Census (2000-01), report on Operational Holdings in Karnataka, Part-I, Directorate of Economics and Statistics and State Agricultural Census Commissioner, Government of Karnataka.

Mr.Somanath, Managing Director of Food Karnataka Limited, reports, "The agri-food scene now is similar to the IT environment in the late '90s, when nobody believe in our state's pioneering venture, like ITPL or IT computer. We are poised on the verge of a similar revolution in food-processing" (Times of India" October, 2004.) The Union Government is partially funding Food park Projects in Karnataka and keeping a benevolent eye on the state in this regard. Currently, the major competitors in food processing are China and India, and both the countries regard food processing as one of the important components of their future economy. Karnataka has already gave an indication of that; the Gherkin (small cucumber) revolution has turned many impoverished farmers into Lakhpathis. This trend is now being replicated in Maharastra and Tamil Nadu Gherkin (baby cucumber) is a much sought after delicacy in the USA and in Europe. Gherkin soaked in vinegar is consumed as a pickle or as a salad ingredient. Its farming has now spread to districts of Hassan, Haveri, and right up to Bagalkot, and is grown exclusively for foreign markets. Currently, Karnataka has a 90 percent share in India's gherkin exports. The six food parks coming up in each of Karnataka's six economic zones-Malur (Kolar), Maddur (Mandya), Hiriyur (Chitradurga), Gangarli (Belgaum), and Jewargi (Gulbarga) and then would mark the next major milestone. Construction work has commenced in these parks and they are expected to be operational in a year. The facilities will have provision for cold storage, grading, processing, etc.

Contracting Farming - Agreement and Farm Management

Contract farming brings together both the firm/company/ private entrepreneurs and farmer for a common goal of getting maximum profits for their investment and agricultural activities respectively. This is to be realized through an agreement. The conditions and provisions included in the agreement/contract is binding on both the parties i.e. firm/company or the private entrepreneur. The agreement or contract is a document stands legal and enforceable depending on the provisions imbibed in it and also with in the framework of law of the land where it is in operation. To execute the provisions of the agreement the concerned organization is bound to set up organizational machinery, which includes manpower with suitable knowledge as required by the agricultural activity undertaken as per the agreement. This organizational machinery is the administrative set-up, which is responsible for smooth functioning of the contract farm.

The wise and right as well timely decisions taken by the administrative set-up yield favorable results generating profits to the contract farm. Any lapses on the part of it land, the contract farm in to losses. Therefore the organizational set-up should have personnel of sound knowledge with administrative as well skill required in their area of work. Thus, as 'Contract Farming' is expanding Farm Management is emerging as an independent discipline. Farm Management deals with organization and operation of a Firm with the objective of maximizing profits from the form business on a continuous basis. It is the science, which deals with the analysis of the farming resources, alternatives, choices, and opportunities within the framework of resource restrictions and social, and personnel constrains of farming business. This complex information is integrated and synthesized to increase profitability of the farming business, the ultimate aim being to raise the standard of living of the farming people. This does not mean that Farm Management deals exclusively with the maximization of income, impact, it takes into account, the goals and objectives of the individual farmer, other than income maximization. Thus, Farm Management is a decision-making science. It helps to decide about the basic course of action of the farming business.

Good farm management can lead to a highly productive use of farm resources and can avail itself of the technological revolution, now going on, in our agriculture. Thus, it can be said that Farm Management is a buzzword for optimizing productivity and farm income. To achieve their goal Firms/ Companies/Private entrepreneurs etc. engaged in contract farming have set-up their own organizational/administrative machinery. However, there are a number of contract farms functioning independently in the country, the administrative machinery constituted, appears to be the same in its structure. One such organizational chart of a famous contract farming company is shown here–

Organizational/Administrative machinery–Chart of the Contract Farming

/

Organizational Chart

/

Co-ordination between Company and Farmer

/

Company

/

Branch Office

/

(Along with collection centers of villages)

/

The Company's Branch Office consists of

/

Area Manager

/

Assistant Production Officer

/

Accountants

/

Field Officers

/

Buyers

/

Buying Assistants

/

Tempo (Locally hired)

Only a few differences are possible to be noticed in the organizational set-up from company/firm to company/firm depending on the crop and other activity undertaken. At different stages of organization, employees are appointed depending upon their job requirements. Sometimes specialized training is imported in addition to their general /specialized education. At higher levels, public relation, customer care and relationship, decision taking and resource management etc are more insisted upon in their training and selection. Their role in the administration is guided and restricted by the agreement of the farm. As an exception and to have a good relationship with the farmers concerned field officers are appointed giving complete preference to local candidates. Field officers act as a facilitators between the company and the farmer, conscious of the company's requirements and expectations from farmers.

The most impartment aspect to be taken into consideration is the "Contract" or "Agreement." This document is the basic instrument in the management of the farm. This must contain facts in specific terms with regard to area committed(Quantity), price or compensation i.e. fixed or market linked, quality parameters, input supply and terms, monitoring and supervision, mode of payment, penalty clauses of any etc. There should not be any ambiguity in the agreement. The agreement must include clearly the method of enforcement of the provisions of the contract in case of disputes. Generally, "contracts" are made in the language known to the farmer. Presently, in many cases English is employed.

Conclusions

A deep look into the practical side of contract farming in the country. An experience differs from individual farmers to farmers and Firms/Companies to Firms/Companies, Many farmers, Firms, and Companies as well some scholars claim various advantages in favour of Contract Farming. However, it is not possible to deny some disadvantages of Contract Farming. It is suggested that suitable steps are to be taken to formulate policies with regard to the shortcomings of the contract agreements. Particularly relating to the specificity, enforcement aspects, conservation of soil nutrients, and protection against over-usage of Chemical Fertilizers, Pesticides, and Fungicides etc. The future of Contract Farming in the country depends upon the transparency and the enforcements aspects of the Contract Agreement between Firms/Companies/Entrepreneurs and Farmers entering into such Contracts.

For the successful functioning of the contract farms, many recommendations have been made. To mention a few- legislation support for early settlement of disputes between farmers and contracting companies, setting up of a quasi-judicial system to contract enforcement, elimination of red-tapism in import of verities/hybrids for contract farms. Capital subsidy for green house, irrigation, and cold storage. No taxes or duties on import of agri-equipment to be used in a registered contract farming programma, funds for setting up laboratories for soil analysis, crop analysis, quality analysis, and water analysis and many more are noticed.

Positive Future of the Contract Farming

However, contract farming in the country has a positive future. Because the farmer in the system is guard against many risks. Nevertheless, we must remember at the same time soil degradation due to too much use of chemicals, rights of the farmers in protecting their own age old, native crops etc.

Reference

National Bank for Agriculture and Rural Development (NABARD) (1999), News Review, Jan-March, Volume 15 No.l, p.56.

Roth Ilyse Randy (1992), Contract Farming Breeds Big Problems for Growers http;//www.flaginc.org.

Grossman, L.S.(1998), The political Ecology of Bananas: Contract Farming, Peasants and Agrarian Change in the Eastern Caribbean, Chapel Hill and London, University of North Carolina Press.

Joger M.F Win (2000), Food Supply Chains from Productivity toward Quality in Fruit and Vegetables Quality: An Integrated View (eds) Shewfelt L Robert and Bernhard Brucker Technomic Publishing Company Inc.Lancaster.

Deodhar Satish Y (2001), WTO Agreements and Indian Agriculture Retrospection and Prospects in Implications of WTO Agreements and Indian Agriculture, Oxpord and IBH New Delhi.

Dileep, B.K, R K Grover and K.N.Rai (2002), Contract Farming in Tomato: An Economic Analysis, Indian Journal of Agricultural Economics, April-June Vol.57, No.2.

www.yahoo.co.in

Miller, L. 1995.. Agribusiness, Contract Farers and Lanfd-Use Sustaiability in North- West Tasmania, in Australian Geographer, No.(26(2),p. 104-111